Faithful
Love

SELWYN HUGHES

Faithful Love

POCKET DEVOTIONS

CWR

January/February
Unveiled Faces

March/April
Our Lord at Prayer

May/June
A Fresh Look at the Church

July/August
The Blessed Life

September/October
Life Convictions

November/December
Surprised by God

The silent Sculptor

FOR READING AND MEDITATION
2 CORINTHIANS 3:1–18

'And we, who with unveiled faces all reflect the Lord's glory, are being transformed into his likeness …' (v.18)

Today, as we begin a new year and open a new chapter in our lives, it seems fitting to set for ourselves a spiritual goal. I suggest this: *to be more like Jesus than we have ever been before.* The picture the apostle Paul presents is breathtaking. We stand with unveiled faces continuously gazing at Christ (that is, giving Him our attention and love), and as we do, we ourselves are changed into His likeness – in fact, we are transformed more and more and with increasing glory. This transformation into Christ's image is brought about by the Holy Spirit, who is the silent Sculptor. Do you know of anything more wonderful than this?

Father, often my gaze has oscillated from one thing to another. This year, please help me to keep my focus on Jesus. May the reflection of His face be seen in mine. Amen.

What a getting!

FOR READING AND MEDITATION
ROMANS 8:28–39

'For those God foreknew he also predestined to be
conformed to the likeness of his Son ...' (v.29)

The verse we looked at yesterday, which will form the basis of our meditations over the next two months – 'we ... with unveiled faces all reflect the Lord's glory' – presents the truth that transformation is continuous. The biblical teaching that we should turn our attention from ourselves to Christ contains a principle that psychologists now accept. They have realised that when we look beyond ourselves to another person we are freed from self-preoccupation – a disease as deadly as cancer. There is a law in psychology that says: whatever gets your attention gets you. If Christ gets our attention then we, in turn, get Him. And what a getting!

Father, draw me from the poisonous centre of myself to the healing centre of Yourself so I become more and more like You. Amen.

'Do you keep stationery here?'

FOR READING AND MEDITATION
PSALM 34:1–14

'Those who look to him are radiant; their faces are never covered with shame.' (v.5)

One of the most important issues in life is fixing our gaze in the right direction. If we look mainly at ourselves we will become discouraged. If we look only at others we may become distracted. However, if Christ becomes the focus of our attention then the Spirit will help us become more like Him. One woman I heard of went into a shop and asked, 'Do you keep stationery here?' 'No,' replied the proprietor facetiously, 'we keep moving.' Similarly, many these days seem to keep moving from one interest to another and never really focus on anything important. Gazing at the face of Jesus means focusing on His character, His attributes and His qualities as portrayed in the Gospels.

Lord Jesus Christ, may my face show that I belong to You. As I look to You more and more may my face too become radiant. Amen.

What a Christian looks like

FOR READING AND MEDITATION
GALATIANS 1:11–24

'... God ... was pleased to reveal his Son in me so that I might preach him among the Gentiles ...' (vv.15–16)

A Harvard professor was asked what a Christian should look like. He thought for a moment and said, 'Phillips Brooks.' When Phillips Brooks was questioned about the secret of his very effective life, he replied, 'Perhaps, if there is a secret, it is that I find myself as the years come and go with an increasing love for Christ. He holds my heart, my attention, my everything.' Outside his church in Boston, USA, is a statue of him. In my opinion there is a flaw: the figure of Christ standing behind him with His hand on Phillips Brooks' shoulder is much smaller than Brooks. It ought to be the other way round, I think – a big Christ making a small man great.

Father, as the moon reflects the light of the sun, so may I turn my face towards Your Son that Your radiance may be reflected by me. Amen.

Nothing is more glorious ...

FOR READING AND MEDITATION
COLOSSIANS 1:24–29

'... God has chosen to make known ... the glorious riches of
this mystery, which is Christ in you, the hope of glory.' (v.27)

It is time to focus on what exactly Paul has in
mind when he talks about having 'unveiled faces'
(2 Cor. 3:18). The point he is making in the chapter from
which this verse is taken is that unconverted Jews, who
rest their spiritual hope on keeping the law rather than
on the grace of God manifested in Jesus Christ, have a
veil over their minds. However, when anyone turns to
Christ this veil is automatically removed. We can then
stand before the Saviour with no obstruction between
us and Him, and thus reflect like mirrors the glory of
the Lord. Nothing is more glorious or beautiful on this
planet than a person in whom the loveliness of Christ
is seen.

*Great God and Saviour, I live in an era when I have Your
personal living presence. I am so grateful. Amen.*

Crazy Galatians!

FOR READING AND MEDITATION
GALATIANS 3:1–14

'Does God give you his Spirit ... because you observe the law, or because you believe what you heard?' (v.5)

The apostle was clearly furious with the religious leaders in Galatia. But he was angry with the believers too. 'You crazy Galatians!' he exclaimed. 'Have you taken leave of your senses?' (Gal. 3:1, *The Message*). The veil that had covered the Galatians' hearts when the old covenant was read had been removed when they trusted Christ. But now the false teaching of those who claimed faith was not enough was coming between them and Christ and preventing them gazing at Him. Paul's letter to the Galatians was intended to help the believers recover their original freedom, and deals also with the nature of that freedom. Legalism and freedom are opposites.

Father, may I never move away from the fact that it is by grace that I am saved, through faith. Amen.

No price could be higher

FOR READING AND MEDITATION
I PETER 1:13–25

'For … it was not with perishable things … that you were redeemed from the empty way of life handed down to you …' (v.18)

It doesn't cost anything to enter the Christian life, but really no price could be higher for arrogant people to pay. We don't mind an occasional free gift, but we struggle to come to terms with the fact that such a great gift as salvation has to be received without us doing anything other than opening our hands to accept it. We like to feel we have done something to earn our salvation, something to merit it, and we cannot bear the loss of pride involved in discovering that salvation is absolutely free. Acceptance by God, however, does not require any payment from us. The price of our salvation has been paid by Christ on the cross. Nothing more is needed. Nothing.

Father, thank You for giving me such a costly gift as salvation at no cost to myself. I boast only in Your wondrous grace. Amen.

Inner torturers

FOR READING AND MEDITATION
MATTHEW 18:21–35

*'The servant fell on his knees ... "Be patient with me,"
he begged, "and I will pay back everything."' (v.26)*

The servant wanted to pay his debt himself. He never really let the wonder of how much he had been forgiven fill his heart and extend it to others. He did not have a *realised* sense of forgiveness. He had an intellectual understanding rather than a heart appreciation and remained hard-hearted. I have observed a similar attitude in the lives of many people. Christ has forgiven them but they still feel they can make some contribution to their salvation, and thus quietly their concept of their redemption from sin changes from something that has been done for them to something they themselves must achieve. When that happens the veil of legalism covers their faces and hinders their spiritual transformation.

O God, if any form of legalism has caused a veil to drop over my face then help me remove it right now. Amen.

Gaining favour with God

'But afterwards they changed their minds and took back the slaves they had freed and enslaved them again.' (v.11)

O ur reading today illustrates how easy it is for us, when our souls are under threat, to depend on doing things that we anticipate will put us in God's good books. When I was a young student approaching exams, I would read an extra chapter of the Bible each day, make sure I gave more than a tithe of my pocket money, and go out of my way to help anyone who appeared to be in need of it. Then, when the exams were over and I was no longer feeling threatened, I changed. The extra things I did before exam time were really 'works of favour'. I was a legalist – depending on 'extras' to give me favour with God.

Father, help me understand that I don't have to do things in order to gain Your favour. Save me from doing right things for the wrong reason. Amen.

Two divine purposes

FOR READING AND MEDITATION
ROMANS 3:9–31

'For we maintain that a man is justified by faith apart from observing the law.' (v.28)

The relationship between law and grace is puzzling to many Christians. Often I have been asked, 'Is the law of God still binding on a Christian?' The answer is, 'Yes and No.' 'No' in the sense that our acceptance by God does not depend on us keeping the law, and 'Yes' in the sense that we are expected to live by the law. Let me put it this way: obedience to the law does not lead to salvation, but salvation leads to obedience to the law. The law says in effect, 'Do this and you will live.' The gospel tells us, 'You live in Christ, so now do this.' The motive has changed – and that is where the difference lies.

Father, how I thank You that though the law said 'Do this and you will live', Jesus Himself has given me life. Now I live in Him. Hallelujah!

Why the law was given

FOR READING AND MEDITATION
ROMANS 7:7–25

'... I would not have known what sin was except through the law.' (v.7)

W hy was the law given in the first place? A simple answer is that it made things worse in order to make them better. The law exposes sin by lifting the lid off so-called respectability and shows us the reality of what lies underneath. The great preachers of the past would always bring the law of God to bear upon people's souls before turning to talk about the grace of God which appeared in Jesus Christ. John Wesley said, 'First I preach the law and then I sprinkle it with grace.' The law no longer operates on its own; it is the Spirit working through the law who brings what we most need – conviction of sin.

Gracious God, thank You that You have hedged me in through the law in order to redeem me. I am saved not by my efforts but by Your beloved Son. Amen.

Humbled – to be exalted

FOR READING AND MEDITATION
I KINGS 8:44–53

'... there is no-one who does not sin ...' (v.46)

John Stott says, 'Not until the law has arrested and imprisoned us will we pine for Christ to set us free. Not until the law has humbled us will we turn to the gospel to raise us to heaven.' The failure to emphasise the law and its purpose has led to us not recognising people as sinners any more. The fact that we are all sinners is not being properly addressed. To attempt to share the gospel without emphasising our sinful state is like casting our pearls before swine. People cannot see the beauty of the pearl because they do not see it set against the ugliness of the sin that is there, deep in every heart.

Father, forgive us if in our efforts to present the gospel we do not tell the full story and ignore sin. Amen.

'Daddy, I love You and ...'

FOR READING AND MEDITATION
JAMES 2:14–26

'What good is it, my brothers, if a man claims to have faith but has no deeds?' (v.14)

Why is it that though we are justified by faith we are told in the New Testament that we will be judged by our works? Our good works are the only public evidence of our faith. Grace touches the springs of our life and love rises as a result – that love working itself out in deeds of kindness. Then, echoing the words of a little boy who had been misbehaving, we say, 'Daddy, I love You, and I'm going to do something about it.' The doing springs out of the loving, and the loving springs out of surrender to Christ. We are saved by faith alone. However, the faith that saves is not alone; it is expressed in good deeds.

Father, Your love for me has inspired my love for You. Now I'm going to do something to show my love. Please give me Your strength and empowerment. Amen.

Integrity is essential

FOR READING AND MEDITATION
1 CHRONICLES 29:10–20

'I know, my God, that you test the heart and are pleased with integrity.' (v.17)

Another matter that will hinder our spiritual transformation is *pretence*, which is a failure to be open and honest. Jeremy Taylor (a seventeenth-century writer) claimed that the first rule for an effective spiritual life is 'Don't lie to yourself, to others, or to God.' In my experience, there is a great deal of pretence amongst the people of God. For example, some Christians pretend they are not hurting when deep down they really are. But, as I have said many times before, integrity requires that whatever is true has to be acknowledged. Some even turn their backs on the Christian life altogether as a result of the disappointment they feel when their experience does not accord with their expectation.

Father, make me a person who is completely honest in thought, attitude and word. In Jesus' name I pray. Amen.

Walking in the truth

FOR READING AND MEDITATION
2 JOHN vv. 1–13

'Grace, mercy and peace from God the Father and from Jesus Christ ... will be with us in truth and love.' (v.3)

There are many believers who pretend the Christian life does more for them than Scripture claims it will. And some go as far as attempting to hold God to promises He never made. The world would listen to us more readily, I believe, if we were not given to making exaggerated statements about the Christian life and pretending that becoming a Christian frees people of their troubles. When I visit churches to preach, I still hear young converts testifying, 'When I became a Christian Jesus took all my troubles away.' That didn't happen in my case. Following my conversion I found I had more troubles (a different set of troubles, it is true), but I discovered that Christ was beside me in them all.

Father, help us to walk not only in love but also in truth. For Jesus' sake. Amen.

Accepting others as they are

FOR READING AND MEDITATION
HEBREWS 10:19–25

'... let us encourage one another – and all the more as you see the Day approaching.' (v.25)

Larry Crabb says that 'some churches tend to reward those members who more convincingly create the illusion of intactness by parading them as examples of what every Christian should be'. Sadly, in a number of churches, depressed people are unwelcome; those who are liked are people who are always on top, always bubbling over, and always presenting the image of what is described as 'positive Christianity'. It would be wonderful if we could always be that way. The reality is, however, that some Christians are caught up in struggles that temporarily get them down. What they need at such times is not an exhortation to 'snap out of it', but the encouragement of knowing that they are accepted just as they are.

Father, if we only accept people if they are as we want them to be then please forgive us. Amen.

Heaven now? Really?

FOR READING AND MEDITATION
2 CORINTHIANS 4:7–18

*'For our light and momentary troubles are achieving for us
an eternal glory that far outweighs them all.'* (v.17)

One woman told me the person who led her to Christ
suggested that as a result of her conversion she
would experience the same intensity of joy here on earth
as she will in heaven. When she didn't she considered
leaving the Church. We do have Christ's joy here and
now, but we also have earth's pain. The teaching that
perfect bliss can be our experience here on earth distorts
what it means to live in a fallen world and as part of an
imperfect, and sometimes evil, community. Those who
pretend that they feel now what they cannot really feel
until they arrive in heaven are tampering with reality
They set themselves and the Church in a false light.

*Father, please save me from escaping into unreality – the
place where truth is compromised. In Jesus' name. Amen.*

No escape from 'groaning'

FOR READING AND MEDITATION
ROMANS 8:18–27

'... we ourselves ... groan inwardly as we wait eagerly
for our adoption as sons ...' (v.23)

I am not denying that we can experience a deep and
wonderful joy here in our present state. However,
that joy is not intended to relieve us of all our troubles;
rather, the joy that comes from fellowship with Christ
and from the hope we have of future glory strengthens
us in life's struggles. In the passage before us today Paul
tells us that we 'groan inwardly as we wait eagerly for
our adoption as sons'. In a fallen world there can be no
escape from 'groaning'. There is no way back into the
Garden of Eden where, before the Fall, all was perfect
bliss. Now, because of the Fall, we either 'groan' or
pretend we don't.

*Father, I see there is no escape from 'groaning'; may it whet
my appetite for heaven. Amen.*

Three groans

FOR READING AND MEDITATION
2 CORINTHIANS 5:1–5

*'For while we are in this tent, we groan and are
burdened …' (v.4)*

P aul mentions three groans in quick succession.
(1) The whole creation groans (Rom. 8:22); (2) we
ourselves groan (Rom. 8:23); (3) the Spirit Himself makes
intercession for us with groans which words cannot
express (Rom. 8:26). There is a groan in creation caused by
sin, there is a groan in the heart of the Christian brought
about by our desire to be rid of this world and to enjoy
the blessings of heaven, and there is also a groan uttered
by the Holy Spirit. To have both joy and an inward groan
is the tension in which all Christians live. We experience
the joy that comes from our personal salvation and our
relationship with Christ, and the groan that comes from
our desire for our bodies to be redeemed.

*Father, looking around I feel despair, looking within I feel
concern, but when I look up I feel hope. Amen.*

Jeremiah – a man of integrity

FOR READING AND MEDITATION
JEREMIAH 20:7–13

'O Lord, you deceived me, and I was deceived; you overpowered me and prevailed.' (v.7)

For one more day we reflect on the need to face everything and everyone with absolute honesty and integrity. Jeremiah is a good example of someone who did this. He deals with the confusion in his heart by confessing to God exactly how he feels. Some people even express surprise that God did not strike Jeremiah dead for daring to address Him in such impertinent language. But I believe God would much rather we be honest than pretend to be what we are not. He will graciously overlook our form of words as He is more concerned about the honesty in our hearts. I make the point again: pretence comes between us and Christ and hinders our spiritual development.

Lord Jesus Christ, again I pray that I might gaze constantly at Your unveiled face with no pretence obscuring my vision – with no pretence in my life. Amen.

'The whole meaning'

FOR READING AND MEDITATION
LUKE 23:26–43

'Jesus said, "Father, forgive them, for they do not know what they are doing."' (v.34)

Along with the other matters we have been considering that prevent us seeing Christ clearly, one of the most damaging to spiritual transformation is this: *an unforgiving spirit*. The prayer of Jesus on the cross embodies the most sublime spirit in this world – the forgiveness of injury and hurt. When, many years ago, a Japanese dissident by the name of Tokichi Ishii was awaiting his death in prison, he came across this prayer of Jesus. In a flash he saw the whole meaning of Christianity. 'That verse,' he said, 'pierced my heart like a five-inch nail.' The pastor who guided me in my youth used to claim that the distinguishing mark of a Christian is a willingness to forgive hurts and injuries.

Lord Jesus Christ, You held no resentment against those who ill-treated You. May Your love so fill me that germs of resentment cannot live in me. Amen.

The secret of forgiving

FOR READING AND MEDITATION
LUKE 7:36–50

'... her many sins have been forgiven – for she loved much.
But he who has been forgiven little loves little.' (v.47)

An interesting observation I have made, having counselled thousands of Christians struggling with the issue of forgiving those who have hurt or injured them, is that *the ones who have been forgiven much find it far easier to forgive others.* The great secret of being willing to forgive others is to focus first on the extent to which you yourself have been forgiven. But, you say, 'I was not a great sinner and never got involved in serious sin. My sins were quite minor ones.' I say, 'No, your problem is you don't realise how much you have been forgiven.' Remember this: there are no little sins because there is no little God to sin against!

Father, help me see clearly how heinous was my sin and how marvellous Your forgiveness, and let me pass forgiveness on to others. Amen.

Leaving room for God's wrath

FOR READING AND MEDITATION
ROMANS 12:9–21

'Do not take revenge, my friends, but leave room for God's wrath …' (v.19)

It may be that deep down people do not want to give up the feeling of power that comes with holding resentment against a person who has hurt them. Resentment and anger are strong feelings, and give one a sense of power and control. Forgiveness involves giving up this sense of control, and leaves us with a feeling of helplessness. We have to depend on God to deal in His own way with any judgment due to the person who has wronged us. Paul explains why we are not to seek revenge. He tells us to 'leave room for God's wrath'. In other words, we should let God handle matters.

Lord Jesus Christ, help me to forgive as graciously as You forgave me and please deliver me from the urge for power and control. Amen.

Not a biblical option!

FOR READING AND MEDITATION
LUKE 6:27–36

'But I tell you who hear me: Love your enemies, do good to those who hate you …' (v.27)

Personal vengeance is not a biblical option. The Christian gospel not only teaches us to refrain from wreaking revenge but goes further and encourages us to do good to the person who has wronged us. By words and deeds we are to show our enemies the responses that typify the gospel. What does an enemy expect, assuming they know they have intentionally hurt or injured us? They expect to be treated in the same way that they have treated us. Goodness, however, whether it is expressed in words or deeds, surprises a heart in which there is evil because it does not fight according to the principles of brute force, power, intimidation and shame but according to the power of love.

Father, may I no longer be influenced by the way others act. Help me to do what You would do if You were me. Amen.

'I *won't* forgive'

FOR READING AND MEDITATION
MATTHEW 6:1–14

'For if you forgive men when they sin against you, your heavenly Father will also forgive you.' (v.14)

We must face the fact that when a Christian says 'I can't forgive' then fundamentally what he or she is saying is 'I *won't* forgive.' God gives every Christian the ability to do whatever He asks of us, and if we refuse to forgive we are going against His instructions to us in the Scriptures and thus putting ourselves in spiritual peril. Your past sins have been pardoned. But your unwillingness to forgive another person is a sin which God cannot forgive since, in order to be forgiven, you must be ready to forgive. And as a result, your fellowship with Christ can be broken. I implore you. By God's grace you will forgive others, won't you?

Father, since I belong to You, how can I harbour an unforgiving spirit? If I am then I am dishonouring your name please forgive me and cleanse me. Amen.

Forgiving and forgetting

FOR READING AND MEDITATION
LUKE 11:1–13

'Forgive us our sins, for we also forgive everyone who sins against us.' (v.4)

Some Christians, when challenged to forgive, say, 'Well, I will forgive, but I can't forget.' Think about that statement in the light of the words of the Lord's Prayer: 'Forgive us our sins, for we also forgive everyone who sins against us.' In effect they are saying, 'I forgive the one who has sinned against me, but I won't forget. Now, Father, forgive me in the same way; forgive me but don't *forget* my sins. When I do something wrong, call attention to my past wrongdoing.' God cannot forgive in that way. He blots out our sin and promises to remember it no more (see Jer. 31:34). Resentment is a physical, mental and spiritual poison. Make sure it does not have a lodging place in your heart.

Lord Jesus, You who forgave those who nailed You to a cross, please help me now to open my heart to Your forgiveness and to forgive others in the same way. Amen.

Resentment is poison

FOR READING AND MEDITATION
COLOSSIANS 3:1–14

'… forgive whatever grievances you may have against
one another. Forgive as the Lord forgave you.' (v.13)

A medical doctor who is a friend of mine once told
me, 'Many of the physical symptoms I see in my
office are really the involuntary confessions of hidden
resentment.' Let me finish this section on an unforgiving
spirit by saying that sad though it is to see a person
crippled physically by an unwillingness to forgive, it is
even sadder to see the inner crippling of the soul when
this is so. If you have an unforgiving spirit then ask God
to free you from it at once. Only when our vision is not
being obscured by something sinful will we be able to
gaze at Christ. And only when we gaze constantly at
Him with unveiled faces will we be transformed into His
likeness.

Father, I acknowledge that we are made for love and not
resentment. Amen.

The me-first syndrome

FOR READING AND MEDITATION
MATTHEW 10:32–42

*'Whoever finds his life will lose it, and whoever loses his
life for my sake will find it.' (v.39)*

Now we start to look at another matter that hinders
our spiritual transformation – *self-centredness*.
This is what has been called the 'me-first syndrome'.
Although many Christians have too low an opinion of
themselves, there are many more who have too high an
opinion of themselves. Self-esteem is fine if it is balanced,
but so few get the balance right. We are told to love
our neighbours as ourselves (Mark 12:31), but some of
us love ourselves too much. Idolatry of any type is an
offence to God, but there is no idolatry as offensive as
the idolatry of the self. Christ was totally devoid of self-
centredness; His whole life was characterised by prayer
and love – by giving out to others.

*Father, I long to be a Christ-controlled person rather than
a self-controlled one. Please help me change my attitude.
Amen.*

The happiest people on earth

FOR READING AND MEDITATION
PHILIPPIANS 2:1–18

'Do nothing out of selfish ambition or vain conceit, but in humility consider others better than yourselves.' (v.3)

We see the apostle Paul cutting right across the cult of the self as he instructs us to look out for the interests of others, regarding them as more important than ourselves. In all my years as a minister of Jesus Christ and a counsellor I have never once seen a happy self-centred person. The self-centred are the self-disrupted. The human personality was designed to have Christ at the centre. If we will not live with Christ at the centre then we will not be able to live with ourselves. I disagree with the psychologists of today who claim that the ego is the centre of the personality. The truth is that we were created to function with God and His Son Jesus Christ at the centre.

O God, I see that only You can set me free to love others and myself in a healthy and balanced way. Amen.

'Where do you think you are?'

FOR READING AND MEDITATION
LUKE 14:25–35

'If anyone comes to me and does not hate … even his own life – he cannot be my disciple.' (v.26)

L ife will tend to leave you 'in knots' if you are self-centred. But if you think of others more highly than you think of yourself then you will become a useful and contributive person. We cannot be made into Christ's image unless we reflect His glory, and self-centredness prevents that. There is an apocryphal story told of a man who had the power to acquire anything he wanted just by saying the word. If he wanted a beautiful house, there it was. If he wanted a beautiful car, there it was. In time, though, he became bored. He wanted to suffer something, to achieve something. So he called out to God for help and said, 'I would rather be in hell than in this place.' A voice answered from the skies, 'Where do you think you are?'

Father, I am convinced that when life is centred on You it is fruitful, when it is centred on myself it is frustrating. Amen.

'Yes, you are very selfish'

FOR READING AND MEDITATION
PSALM 119:33–40

'Turn my heart towards your statutes and not towards selfish gain.' (v.36)

Not only does the Bible stress the importance of refusing to be self-centred, this principle is found also in the design of our physical beings. Take the basis of life, the cell. Each cell of our bodies serves the whole body, not itself. A cell that does not serve others becomes a cancer which breaks the law of being and ends in death. While Dr William Sadler, a well-known psychiatrist, was counselling a woman, she said, 'I am very sensitive.' 'Yes,' answered Dr Sadler, 'you are very selfish.' 'But I didn't say "selfish",' she retorted. 'No, but I did,' said the doctor. This woman went away angry, but came back for her next appointment with a changed attitude.

Father, if selfishness is deeply rooted in me then remove it I pray. Make me a truly other-centred person. Amen.

The royal law

FOR READING AND MEDITATION
JAMES 2:1–13

'If you really keep the royal law found in Scripture, "Love your neighbour as yourself," you are doing right.' (v.8)

There are some believers who have the idea that as Christians they must love others but not themselves. This is not what the Bible teaches. A healthy self-love is legitimate and right. Those who love others and not themselves allow others to sap the life out of them. There must be balance. If we act as if we have no love for ourselves then self-love will dress itself up in other guises and negatively affect all our relationships. I recall the times when I have been unduly nervous before giving a talk. Always this has happened because I was thinking more of myself and how I would come across than the content of the message. We function best when we think of something or someone other than ourselves.

Lord Jesus Christ, You whose actions were completely other-centred, grant that I will be transformed and act in a similar manner. Amen.

'If you *knew* my centre'

FOR READING AND MEDITATION
COLOSSIANS 3:1–17

'When Christ, who is your life, appears, then you also will appear with him in glory.' (v.4)

J.B. Phillips translates part of today's text in this way: 'Christ, the secret centre of our lives'. 'Nothing,' says the writer Ian Macpherson, 'moves in the material universe save in relation to some regulative centre. From the planet spinning round its sun to the electron waltzing round the proton in the atom, the world is full of illustrations of the working of this law.' It is the same in our moral and spiritual lives. Everything turns upon some regulative centre. That centre may be one of a number of things; it may be the pursuit of wealth, the quest for truth, or the passionate love of beauty. For a Christian, however, the centre of our lives must be Jesus Christ.

Lord, how grateful I am that the centre of my life has changed and that You are now the centre. Amen.

Just one word!

FOR READING AND MEDITATION
1 CORINTHIANS 10:23–33

'Nobody should seek his own good, but the good of others.' (v.24)

A few years ago I was looking at some gravestones in a churchyard. One particular stone caught my attention. The middle names of the man buried there took up about five lines of the stone followed by a long list of his awards and degrees. As I tried to take in all this man's names and awards a text floated into my mind: 'You are to give him the name Jesus' (Matt. 1:21). Just one word! But that one word has become the Word. Almost one third of the world bows before Him. I cannot remember any one of the names of the person buried in the churchyard, but how can I forget the name of the Man who put the needs of others before His own, and lived and died demonstrating such self-sacrificing love?

Gracious Lord and Master, I recognise my need of Your help in maintaining a life of Christ-centredness. Amen.

When bigotry banishes love

FOR READING AND MEDITATION
LUKE 9:46–50

'Master … we saw a man driving out demons … and we tried to stop him, because he is not one of us.' (v.49)

Another matter that may prevent us seeing Christ clearly and thus prevent the light from His countenance being reflected by us is – *religious bigotry*. Over the years I have been astonished at the number of Christians I have met (and sometimes still do) who are intolerant of those who belong to a different Christian church or denomination. In recent years there have been positive moves to deal with this problem, but there are still far too many Christians who are suspicious of those who do not belong to the same church group or denomination. Our Lord did not hold such an attitude. And neither must we. I do not believe God is against our denominations. In my opinion He just ignores them.

Father, help me understand that when I belong to You I belong to everyone else who belongs to You. Amen.

'Headed for sure damnation'

FOR READING AND MEDITATION
MATTHEW 22:34–40

'Love your neighbour as yourself.' (v.39)

The history of the Christian Church, I am afraid, is punctuated with accounts of one group of Christ's followers ill-treating another group for no other reason than that they were 'not one of us' and even 'headed for sure damnation'. Looking back from the vantage point of the twenty-first century it seems astonishing that during one period Catholics would burn Protestants and then, at another time, Protestants would torture Catholics. And all this was undertaken in the name of Christ who taught us to love our neighbour as ourselves. I have no hesitation in saying that bigotry will hinder the reflection of Christ's love in our lives. Shame on us if such an attitude exists. Decide to be rid of it this very day.

Loving heavenly Father, I ask that You will help me see if there is any religious bigotry in my heart. In Jesus' name. Amen.

Christ's concerned prayer

FOR READING AND MEDITATION
JOHN 17:20–26

'I pray ... for those who will believe in me ... that all of them may be one, Father ...' (vv.20–21)

There is often a lack of tolerance between Calvinists and Arminians, charismatics and non-charismatics, those who believe in baptism by sprinkling and those who believe in baptism by total immersion. Surely love ought to help us to disagree without being disagreeable. When we demonstrate attitudes that do not reflect Christ's character, we are dishonouring His name. In the 40 years during which my writings have been read by people from all sections of the Church, I have strenuously tried to avoid being disrespectful or unduly critical of those who hold different views from myself. My ultimate aim in my writings is not to send people into the day with a bee in their bonnet but a blessing in their heart.

Father, I accept that there will inevitably be disagreements between Your children, but please help us disagree without being disagreeable. Amen.

What lies behind bigotry?

FOR READING AND MEDITATION
EPHESIANS 4:1–16

'Make every effort to keep the unity of the Spirit through the bond of peace.' (v.3)

A colleague once said, 'A bigoted person has a floating anger, and will focus that on anything with which he or she disagrees. If you were to strip down the soul of a bigot you would find at the core a disposition that is fiercely adversarial and lacking in love.' It is suggested that to a large extent temperament determines which type of worship service a person will prefer. Some appreciate a liturgical form of worship whereas others like a more simple form of service with a strong emphasis on the preaching of the Word. However, whatever our temperament, no Christian should regard himself or herself as superior to another. Love provides us with the power to live with differences.

O God, give me the same love for those who make up Your Church as You have. I ask this in Jesus' name. Amen.

No other way

FOR READING AND MEDITATION
I JOHN 3:11–24

*'Anyone who hates his brother is a murderer, and you
know that no murderer has eternal life in him.' (v.15)*

The real problem which lies in the heart of a bigot is
a lack of Christian love. Bigots claim to stand for the
right, but the attitude in which they do so is wrong.
When I was a pastor I would sometimes hear one person
say to another, 'Now I'm telling you this in love.' It was
quite evident, however, that love was non-existent.
There might have been truth, but the effectiveness of the
truth was cancelled out because no love was present,
and when love is absent hate can quickly fill the heart.
What, then, are we to do when someone is contentious?
We are to go on loving. We must meet slander with
affection, scorn with service, and pride with humility.
There is no other way.

*O God, it is not easy to go on loving in the face of contempt
and slander. Please give me Your love for others. Amen.*

FEBRUARY 9

How long ...?

FOR READING AND MEDITATION
ACTS 4:23–37

*'With great power the apostles continued to testify to
the resurrection ... and much grace was upon them all.'*
(v.33)

There is a church, I am told, in southern England,
which once had a dividing wall. In this church the
nave was Anglican and the chancel Roman Catholic.
The division occurred in the sixteenth century when
Henry VIII broke with Rome. It took centuries for that
wall to be removed, just as it has taken centuries for the
walls between the people of God to start coming down.
But coming down they are – a fact that ought to stir
our hearts in praise of God. How long, I wonder, will it
take for Christ's dismembered Body to be made whole
again – as it was in the days following Pentecost? Not
long, perhaps, if the Church turns its face determinedly
against all bigotry.

*O God, forgive us for dismembering Your Body by our splits
and factions. Help us stamp out all bigotry. In Christ's
name. Amen.*

One shepherd – one flock

FOR READING AND MEDITATION
JOHN 10:1–21

'They too will listen to my voice, and there shall be one flock and one shepherd.' (v.16)

In a small town in the United Kingdom there is a church known to me where the Roman Catholic congregation and the Protestant congregation share the same building. A curtain is drawn across the Roman Catholic altar at the conclusion of the mass, and as the worshippers leave they say 'good morning' to the Protestant worshippers who are making their way into the church. The two congregations mingle with each other and sometimes drink coffee together. It does not seem strange to them. It may seem strange to those who are bigoted, but not to those who do this. Let us never forget we have one Shepherd and we are one flock.

O God, Your Son prayed that all Your people might be one as You and He are one. Forgive us that we Your Church, show to the world a broken image of Your face. Forgive and restore us. Amen.

Wholehearted commitment

FOR READING AND MEDITATION
MATTHEW 6:25–34

'But seek first his kingdom and his righteousness, and all these things will be given to you as well.' (v.33)

Another matter that will hinder us from being spiritually transformed is – *a divided mind*. By this I mean when we are not wholehearted in our commitment to Christ – when we want Him but we want something else more. It was said of King Jotham in the Old Testament that he 'grew powerful because he walked steadfastly before the LORD his God' (2 Chron. 27:6). But of another king, Amaziah, we read, 'He did what was right in the eyes of the LORD, but not wholeheartedly' (2 Chron. 25:2). A divided mind was his undoing. Later a conspiracy was formed against Amaziah which brought about his assassination at Lachish. Inner division led to outer disloyalty, and that, in turn, led to his death.

Lord Jesus Christ, Your single-minded devotion to Your Father's will brought You poise, peace and power. I long to be like You. Amen.

No cement in wrongdoing

FOR READING AND MEDITATION
NUMBERS 32:1–24

'But if you fail to do this, you will be sinning against the LORD; and you may be sure that your sin will find you out.' (v.23)

A life that is being lived at cross purposes and is not wholehearted will not reflect the Lord's glory, and we will not be transformed into His likeness with ever-increasing glory. No one can afford to hold any inner conflict. Christians must throw themselves on the right side of every issue – the biblical side. The worst thing about any kind of wrongdoing is being the one who is doing the wrong. There is no cement in wrongdoing! It will not hold together. Often people misquote today's text and say, 'Be sure your sin will be found out.' But notice again what it says: 'Be sure that your sin will find you out.' It will find you out through inner irritation, unhappiness, frustration, and other forms of misery.

Father, may my commitment to You be so wholehearted that it will determine every other commitment. Amen.

Not 'will not' but 'cannot'

FOR READING AND MEDITATION
LUKE 11:14–28

'Any kingdom divided against itself will be ruined, and a house divided against itself will fall.' (v.17)

You will no doubt have heard the saying 'United we stand, divided we fall'. It could also be expressed in this way: 'Inwardly united we stand, inwardly divided we fall'. Jesus tells us that a house divided against itself cannot stand. This is something acknowledged by modern psychology. One psychologist says, 'There may be a score of active motives, but they must all harmonise with one another if we are to live effectively. One may dominate, but the others must co-operate otherwise there will be mutiny.' The effect of inner division is universal. It applies everywhere and to everything – to a kingdom, a family, or an individual. A house divided against itself *cannot* stand. Not will not. *Cannot.*

Father, I see that inner division inevitably brings inner disintegration. Drive this truth more deeply into my spirit I pray. Amen.

A rather strange vision

FOR READING AND MEDITATION
ZECHARIAH 5:5–11

*'He said, "This is wickedness," and he pushed her back
into the basket and pushed the lead cover down over its
mouth.' (v.8)*

To be transformed into Christ's likeness we must
make sure that inner division does not prevent us
gazing at Him. Resolve any inner conflict in your life right
away. There is one thing above all others that causes
breakdowns in people: a conflict. And there is one thing
above all others that can end a conflict: surrendering it
to God. But first the conflict must be acknowledged. We
often push our conflicts down into the basket of the
subconscious, put the lid on them and hope we have
dealt with them. But they go to work there as a hidden
complex. If you have any inward conflicts, surrender
them now into God's hands. Believe me, your conflicts
are better in His hands than in yours.

*O living Christ, You who commanded the waves to be still,
speak to any clamorous voices there may be in me and bid
them cease. Amen.*

Going all out for Jesus

FOR READING AND MEDITATION
2 CORINTHIANS 5:6–10

'So we make it our goal to please him, whether we are at home in the body or away from it.' (v.9)

All behaviour moves towards a goal. If you want to know why a person behaves the way he or she does then ask yourself: What is the goal behind the behaviour? In our text today the apostle Paul tells us that his overarching goal in life was to please Christ. You can be sure of this: when we are totally and wholeheartedly committed to pleasing God then our personality will be healthy. We are at our best physically, psychologically and spiritually when, like Paul, we make it our overall goal to please Christ. Let me urge you today to go all out for Jesus. Don't be a person with mixed motives, trying to please God one moment and then trying to please yourself the next.

Lord Jesus, just as Your great goal in life was to please the Father so may I make it my great goal to please You, so surrendered to You that I surrender to nothing else. Amen.

Knowing God or using Him?

FOR READING AND MEDITATION
MATTHEW 20:20–28

'Grant that one of these two sons of mine may sit at your right and the other at your left in your kingdom.' (v.21)

In Matthew 27:56 we are told that this mother was one of the women who sometimes travelled with Jesus and helped to look after Him. Was she a woman with mixed motives – waiting on Jesus but at the same time wanting something for her two sons? Dr Larry Crabb has written, 'For many modern-day Christians our relationship with God is not about knowing Him but using Him. I have felt for years that most of us in American Christianity use God to solve our problems rather than using our problems to know more of God.' If our dominant motive is to get God to do things for us, and not to know Him better, then deep down we are more interested in what God can do for us than in what we can do for Him.

Father, if my dominant interest in relating to You is to get You to do things for me, then please forgive me and restore me. Amen.

An all-out commitment

FOR READING AND MEDITATION
LUKE 11:33–36

'When your eyes are good, your whole body also is full of light.' (v.34)

We are made for unity, for integrity, for wholeness. When we lack singleness of purpose the result is divided loyalties. God originally willed unity for our personalities, but it is not enough that this is what He wills – we must will it too. Not just wish for it, but *will* it. So throw your whole will on the side of inward unification. Decide that what you really want is single-minded devotion and dedication to Christ, and then give yourself to pursuing this wholeheartedly and without any reservations. When our eyes are good (that is, clear), then our whole body will be full of light and the blood of Jesus Christ will continuously cleanse us from all sin, all division, all double-mindedness. You will be free.

O God, help me to be clear and wholehearted in my commitment to You. In Jesus' name I pray. Amen.

Alien to a Christian

FOR READING AND MEDITATION
PHILIPPIANS 4:10–20

'I can do everything through him who gives me strength.'
(v.13)

Another matter that can prevent Christ's transforming power reaching us is looking at Him, and at life in general, with *a negative attitude*. I had a friend whose first reaction to anything new was always 'No'. He objected to everything and so his life was frustrated when it could have been fruitful. When Pharaoh refused to let the Israelites leave Egypt: 'Dense swarms of flies poured into Pharaoh's palace ... the land was ruined by the flies' (Exod. 8:24). The lives of the Egyptians were made a misery by such tiny things as flies. Negativism may seem a small matter but, believe me, many a life has been ruined because of it. Negative attitudes ought to be as alien to a Christian as a thorn is to the flesh.

O God, if I am a negative person then change my attitude I pray. In Jesus' name. Amen.

Negatives to positives

FOR READING AND MEDITATION
LUKE 15:1–10

'But the Pharisees and the teachers of the law muttered, "This man welcomes sinners ..."' (v.2)

Jesus was positive in His approach to everything. He was criticised because He ate with tax collectors and sinners – the implication being that He was like them. That attitude was very negative so how did He meet it? With another negative? No, instead He told three parables – the lost sheep, the lost coin, and the lost son. He gave a positive presentation of the seeking love of God. The new faith He was about to launch would turn negative situations to positive. He did that right up to the end of His life on earth, winning positives out of negatives. The cross was the greatest negative that confronted Him but He turned it into the greatest positive the world has ever known.

O Father, I am so thankful I am linked to Your Son who can bring a positive out of a negative. May I be like Him. Amen.

A thousand times – Yes!

FOR READING AND MEDITATION
2 CORINTHIANS 1:12–22

'For the Son of God … was not "Yes" and "No", but in him it has always been "Yes".' (v.19)

Jesus was expert at winning positives out of negatives. He has been called 'The Great Affirmation'. But perhaps nothing underlines the positivity of Jesus more than our text for today. Without Christ life has to be expressed with a 'No' rather than a 'Yes'. The English philosopher Bertrand Russell remarked, 'Life is a bottle of very nasty wine that leaves a bad taste in the mouth.' And Jean-Paul Sartre declared, 'Hell is other people.' When a famous actor was dying he said, 'There is no reality; it is all a farce. Let down the curtain, the farce is over.' Over against all these 'Nos' a divine 'Yes' has sounded in Christ. Does He affirm all the promises of God? Yes! Yes! A thousand times – Yes!

O Father, how thankful I am that in a world where there are so many 'Nos' I have found a divine 'Yes' – 'The Great Affirmation'. Amen.

The poor person

FOR READING AND MEDITATION
HEBREWS 13:1–8

'Jesus Christ is the same yesterday and today and for ever.' (v.8)

If you have a negative philosophy of life you will end up a poor person – poor, that is, in terms of your expectations of life. The point I made yesterday about Jesus being the 'Yes' to life means we have to live by affirmation, not negation. We must say 'No' to some things, of course, in order to say 'Yes' to the right things. But generally speaking we are made to live by affirmation. We follow the One who brings to pass all the promises of God – promises of a new heart and of eternal life. The urge for life – abundant life – is felt by every single one of us, and Jesus is the divine 'Yes' to that. Our urge for life is met by Him. And how!

O God, please help me turn everything in my life into that which is positive and creative. Let Your awakening, stimulating hand always be on my spirit. In Jesus' name. Amen.

History has forgotten them

FOR READING AND MEDITATION
MARK 7:1–23

'The Pharisees ... who had come from Jerusalem ... saw some of his disciples eating food with hands that were ... unwashed.' (vv.1–2)

Like the Pharisees we have read about today, there are a number of people whose whole lives are governed by negatives. These men had travelled all the way from Jerusalem to meet Him but their attitude was so negative that all they could see was unwashed hands. They failed to notice the unique work of redemption that was being undertaken right before their eyes in the Person of Jesus. All they saw was an infringement of rituals. History has forgotten the scribes and Pharisees who were there that day except as a backdrop to the positive Christ. If we refused to speak until we could speak words that are positive how different our life, and the world of our relationships, would be!

Father, help me seal my lips to negativism and doubt, and unseal them to faith. In Jesus' name. Amen.

Chewing on bones

FOR READING AND MEDITATION
MATTHEW 7:1–5

'For in the same way as you judge others, you will be judged …' (v.2)

A minister was falsely accused by a woman of not believing in the virgin birth. The minister made a special announcement in his church stating that he certainly did believe in the virgin birth. The woman who had made the accusation was present in the congregation and heard what he said. Despite this she then went out and argued, 'Yes, he did say he believed in the virgin birth, but he didn't say Jesus was born of the Virgin Mary.' How sad. Some people are even troubled if you take away the bones on which they habitually chew in order to perpetuate their negativism. That woman would not change until she acknowledged her problem. No acknowledgement of the problem, no change of the problem. Period.

Father, help me relate to others with a more positive attitude. In Jesus' name. Amen.

The affirmative side

FOR READING AND MEDITATION
2 CORINTHIANS 2:1–17

'But thanks be to God, who always leads us in triumphal procession in Christ ...' (v.14)

Christians ought to be the most positive people on the planet because we belong to the Creator whose purposes for His creation are positive. Paul had an amazingly positive attitude but most of us would have described his life as a constant procession of trouble, not triumph. Later, Paul reminds the Corinthians of the numerous times he was imprisoned, flogged, threatened with death, shipwrecked, and endured hunger and thirst (2 Cor. 11:23–28). God, however, enabled Paul to make the trouble into a triumph, the negative into a positive. Paul rescued out of the heart of every death situation a life contribution. And so, my dear friend, can you. With God you can come out on the affirmative side of every situation.

Father, if I have been responding to life negatively then please help me to change my outlook. In Jesus' name. Amen.

'More than a reflection'

FOR READING AND MEDITATION
I CORINTHIANS 13:1–13

'Now we see but a poor reflection as in a mirror ...' (v.12)

The Christian whose gaze is set on the Lord becomes like a mirror in which the image of Jesus is seen more and more clearly. Yet we do more than just reflect Christ's glory. We are changed into the same image which we see in the mirror – we are *transformed* into it. Christians who gaze at Christ with no veil on their face are continuously being transformed into His likeness. A mirror, to serve its purpose, needs to keep still before the one using it. Keeping still before the Lord is half the secret of reflecting His beauty. We keep still in adoring worship before Christ – the Holy Spirit does the rest.

Lord Jesus, I see that when I gaze on You the reward is beyond all telling. I am changed from one degree of glory to another. Amen.

Is God the initiator?

FOR READING AND MEDITATION
I TIMOTHY 3:1–16

'He appeared in a body ... was believed on in the world, was taken up in glory.' (v.16)

I have headed this page: 'Is God the initiator?' And now for the answer: He is. Listen to this. Let it take your breath away. Jesus Christ was transformed into our image so that we might be transformed into His. The incarnation is the miracle of miracles. God became like us in order that we might become like Him. The first step to transformation is to receive Jesus Christ into your heart and life by confessing your sins and receiving His forgiveness. Have you done that? If not then, as His ambassador and representative, I beg you to do so now. Pray this prayer and mean what you say:

Lord Jesus Christ, please forgive my sin and make me Your child. As I reach up to You I know You are reaching down to me. I receive You now as my Lord and Saviour. Amen.

Adoring contemplation

FOR READING AND MEDITATION
PSALM 27:1–14

'One thing I ask of the LORD ... that I may dwell in the house of the LORD ... to gaze upon the beauty of the LORD ...' (v.4)

On 1 January I said that gazing at Christ means giving Him our attention and love. Godly men and women of the past claimed that the secret of being transformed into Christ's image is to sit before Him in adoring contemplation. This goes beyond prayer, petition, intercession, thanksgiving and praise. Although prayer and praise were important to them, what most contributed to their spiritual transformation was simply looking in love and longing at Christ and adoring Him for who He is. We have to go beyond probing, asking, seeking, or even trying to understand, and simply sit in adoration before Him. Their holiness, they claimed, was a by-product of this. They looked at Christ and He looked at them.

Help me, dear Saviour, not just to pray to You or even just look at You, but to gaze at You. Amen.

'I just want to look at You'

FOR READING AND MEDITATION
PSALM 37:1–7

'Be still before the Lord and wait patiently for him …' (v.7)

We remind ourselves of this important thought: we become like that on which we constantly gaze. Since God has unveiled Himself in Jesus, so we, in response, must ensure that nothing comes between us and Him, and gaze at Him in wonder. A mother tells a lovely story about her little boy. One day he went into his father's study, and his father asked him what he wanted. The boy replied, 'I don't want anything. I just want to look at you. You have such a lovely face.' So the boy sat and gazed at his father's lovely face, and in the process, said the mother, he became more and more like him. The more we contemplate Christ, the more we gaze at Him, the more we will become like Him and reflect Him to others.

O God, may I rise to every one of the challenges You have given me over the past days, and be transformed into Your likeness with ever-increasing glory. In Jesus' name I pray. Amen.

Prayer reveals the pray-er

FOR READING AND MEDITATION
JOHN 17:1–26

*'My prayer is not that you take them out of the world but
that you protect them from the evil one.' (v.15)*

There is no better way to prepare our hearts for
the Easter season, I believe, than by a serious
contemplation of the prayer of our Lord found in John 17.
Today we begin by reading the whole prayer, and then we
shall focus on it verse by verse and phrase by phrase. We
can tell a lot about people by the way they pray. What
do we learn about our Lord as we listen to Him pray
within hours of being crucified? One thing we discover
is that though His body would soon be stretched on
a cross, His primary thoughts were not about Himself
but the wellbeing of His disciples. The prayer reveals the
pray-er. And how!

*Father, unfold to me by Your Spirit the riches and depths of
this, my Saviour's prayer. In Jesus' name. Amen.*

Knowing *who* God is

FOR READING AND MEDITATION
LUKE 11:1–13

'When you pray, say: "Father …"' (v.2)

Why is it important to address God as 'Father'? One reason is that it turns our minds away from ourselves to our Father who is in heaven. Then, and only then, can we get the right perspective. Our biggest failures in prayer begin when we rush into God's presence and start presenting our petitions without any regard to *who* God is. The very mention of the word 'Father' helps us understand that we are not engaging in a theological dialogue; we are talking to our Father. And 'Father' is a relationship word; we can't call God 'Father' without acknowledging that we are His children. No prayer can be true prayer unless we understand that when we talk to God we talk to Him as a child talks to a loving father.

O Father, help me never to forget that prayer begins with adoration, not with supplication – with the focus on You, not on me. Amen.

Prayer's first principle

FOR READING AND MEDITATION
2 CORINTHIANS 6:1–18

'I will be a Father to you, and you will be my sons and daughters, says the Lord Almighty.' (v.18)

Some people are uncomfortable with the term 'Father'. Let there be no mistake about it – true Christian prayer is to a Father who has a Father's heart, a Father's love and a Father's compassion. The very first principle of prayer, then, is that we come to God as a child comes to a loving father – in trust, simplicity, and with frankness. A father is a person, not a machine. A father is able to hear, and so is not aloof and insensitive. A father responds, and is therefore interested and concerned. Six times in John 17 our Lord addresses God as Father. And why? Because that was the way He instinctively looked upon Him.

Gracious and loving God, the thought that You are my Father and I am Your child fills me with a joy that I am not able to describe. Amen.

A root problem

FOR READING AND MEDITATION
PSALM 89:14–29

'He will call out to me, "You are my Father, my God, the Rock my Saviour."' (v.26)

As a counsellor, I have tried to help countless numbers of people over the years with the problems they have had concerning prayer. With many people, the root problem is not that they are insincere or lacking in dedication and commitment; the root problem is that they do not have a clear concept of God as Father. Those who do know God in this way are the ones who are most eager to come into His presence and to speak with Him as often as is possible. Let us never forget, then, that our Lord taught us the first principle in prayer is to see God as our Father. Who are we to claim that we know better than Christ?

Gracious and loving God, remove from my heart any misconceptions I may have concerning You, and help me to see You as You really are. Amen.

Right on time

FOR READING AND MEDITATION
ROMANS 5:1–11

'You see, at just the right time, when we were still powerless, Christ died for the ungodly.' (v.6)

We look now at the next words of our Lord in John 17: 'Father, *the time has come*' (v.1). This is not the same as saying, 'My time has come.' '*My* time has come' has about it an air of resignation; '*the* time has come' is more suggestive of realisation. Once Jesus had embarked upon His ministry, His eye seems to have been constantly turned upwards to heaven as if gazing at some celestial clock. Everything He did appears to have been regulated by the tick of its pendulum. And wherever He went and whatever He did, He was always right on time. It should not surprise us, therefore, to find that even as He draws near to the hour of His death, His feet do not drag. He is as punctual as ever. Right on time.

Lord Jesus Christ, You always moved in harmony with Your Father's will. Please enable me to do the same. Amen.

The guided life

FOR READING AND MEDITATION
JOHN 7:25–44

'At this they tried to seize him, but no-one laid a hand on him, because his time had not yet come.' (v.30)

The Jews sought to arrest Jesus in the Temple. But they were unable to bring about their evil purpose because, as John explains, 'his time had not yet come'. However it is important to observe that our Lord never took unnecessary risks and nor was he foolhardy or took the matter of divine protection for granted: His refusal to throw Himself down from the Temple being just one example (Matt. 4:5–7). He received His instructions from His Father through waiting upon Him in prayer. Perhaps if we spent more time in prayer, and thus lived more guided lives, we would avoid the traps the devil sets for our feet.

O Father, help me know You better, for only then can I live a guided life. In Jesus' name I pray. Amen.

When God laughs

FOR READING AND MEDITATION
PSALM 2:1–12

'The One enthroned in heaven laughs; the Lord scoffs at them.' (v.4)

Often we become downcast and depressed as we look at the state of the world and see the Church derided by the men and women of this age. But we must learn that despite all appearances to the contrary, God's hand is upon the whole situation and a divine plan is being worked out. At any moment God can arise and confound His enemies. Why does He laugh? Because as He sees the little people of this earth strutting around so arrogantly, He knows that at a word He could destroy them all. He could, but He won't, for divine purposes are being accomplished. Everything that is happening is being worked out according to God's schedule. His – not ours.

O Father, please give me the divine perspective on all matters. Show me that Your purposes are being worked out even if appearances are to the contrary. Amen.

God is to be glorified

FOR READING AND MEDITATION
PSALM 86:1–17

*'I will praise you, O Lord my God, with all my heart;
I will glorify your name for ever.' (v.12)*

Christ's overwhelming desire in everything He did was to glorify His Father. He lived for that one purpose, and for that one purpose alone. We will never really understand the reason for us being here on this earth until we come to see that the whole purpose of our salvation is that we should glorify the Father. What a difference it would make to our lives if we could fully grasp this. We think more in terms of God glorifying us than of us glorifying Him. Our Lord lived entirely and exclusively for the Father's glory – and so must we. I would say that the most significant sign of our maturity as Christians is whether our all-consuming desire is for God's glory rather than our own. Would you not agree?

Father, help me understand that I am made to glorify You, and the more I do the more my inner being is drawn to health. Your glory is my glory. Amen.

The greatest sin

FOR READING AND MEDITATION
DANIEL 5:17–31

*'But you did not honour the God who holds in his hand
your life and all your ways.' (v.23)*

Why do respectable people who come into our churches have a struggle to believe they are sinners? Because they are under the impression that sin consists of vices such as drunkenness, adultery and dishonesty. If they haven't committed any of these evils they do not think of themselves as 'sinners'. The essence of sin, however, is the failure to glorify God, and anyone who does not glorify God is guilty of the worst kind of sin. Belshazzar's greatest sin was not that he desecrated the holy goblets and filled them with wine for his own enjoyment; his greatest sin was that he did not honour and glorify God. Everyone has to admit to this. Not to do so is a sign of extreme arrogance.

O God, thank You for showing me that my purpose on earth is to glorify You. Help me do so in every way possible. Amen.

'What's in it for me?'

FOR READING AND MEDITATION
COLOSSIANS 3:1–17

'Set your minds on things above, not on earthly things.' (v.2)

I find it deeply moving that immediately before going to the cross, and knowing the pain and agony that lay ahead, our Lord's one desire was this: that He might glorify the Father. He was saying in effect, 'Father, I have come to this earth to bring glory to Your name; strengthen Me so that I will be able to do that.'

How different are our attitudes when called upon to face a crisis. We are more concerned with how we will come out of it than how much God will be glorified. How far removed we are from the time when people cried out, not 'What will Christ do for me?', but 'What can I do for Him?'

O God, we ask Your forgiveness that we are more concerned for our own comfort than we are for Your glory. Wash us by the water of Your Word. Amen.

'Saved in eternity!'

FOR READING AND MEDITATION
EPHESIANS 1:1–14

'And he made known to us the mystery of his will according to his good pleasure, which he purposed in Christ …' (v.9)

The next phrase in John 17 is: 'For you granted him authority over all people that he might give eternal life to all those you have given him' (v.2). These words imply that at some point in the past Christ, the second Person of the Trinity, was placed in a position of authority and assigned the task of giving eternal life to as many as God foreordained. Our salvation is a planned salvation. It is not an afterthought, but was conceived in the mind of the Trinity long before time began. Dr Martyn Lloyd Jones said, 'We were saved in eternity!' One Welsh preacher summed it up: 'God thought it, Christ bought it, the Spirit wrought it, and though the devil fought it – thank God I've got it.'

O God, how I thank You for including me in the glorious plan of salvation. Blessed be Your holy name for ever. Amen.

Jubilant praise

FOR READING AND MEDITATION
REVELATION 5:1–14

'He came and took the scroll from the right hand of him who sat on the throne.' (v.7)

In today's reading we find that at the heart of the universe is a Lamb. Jesus, the Lion of the tribe of Judah, humbled Himself to become the Lamb slain before the foundation of the world. This means that God had a Lamb before He had a man, and the Lamb was waiting to deal with the effects of humanity's fall (see John 1:29). There was a cross set up in eternity before there was a cross set up on the hill called Calvary. The only rightful action to take in the light of these glorious facts is to join in jubilant praise with heaven's chorus and sing, 'Worthy is the Lamb, who was slain, and yet lives again.'

Father, You saw me in my sin and You saw me being delivered from it. All glory be to the Lamb for ever and ever. Amen.

Marked out in eternity

FOR READING AND MEDITATION
JOHN 6:25–40

'All that the Father gives me will come to me, and whoever comes to me I will never drive away.' (v.37)

Running through Scripture is the truth that before the foundation of the world God the Father gave to Christ a special group of people who are destined to enjoy the blessings of salvation and live with Him for ever. God chose them and, according to the verse before us today, God is the One who draws them to Himself. It is as if the Father said to the Son, 'I am giving You a special group of people. I will draw them, and I want You to live in them and transform them for Me.' Our salvation was forethought, foreseen and foreordained. If you are a Christian you are an inheritor of a kingdom that was established before the foundation of the world.

Father, I did not 'accidentally' come to You. I came because I was drawn – drawn by a Power that reached out to me from eternity. Thank You, my Father. Amen.

What exactly is a Christian?

FOR READING AND MEDITATION
1 JOHN 2:18–27

'And this is what he promised us – even eternal life.' (v.25)

People ask, 'What exactly is a Christian?' In my judgment the best and the simplest answer is this: a Christian is someone who has eternal life. This is the primary reason why God sent His Son into the world: 'that he might give eternal life to all those you have given him' (John 17:2). And in John 17:3 our Lord explains just what eternal life is: 'Now this is eternal life: that they may know you, the only true God, and Jesus Christ, whom you have sent.' Eternal life, then, consists in knowing God and God can be truly known only when we approach Him through His Son. Life, real life that is, cannot be found in any way except through Jesus Christ.

O God, help us to be more clear and understandable in our evangelism. In Jesus' name we ask it. Amen.

No place for idols

FOR READING AND MEDITATION
1 JOHN 5:1–21

'Dear children, keep yourselves from idols.' (v.21)

We move on to consider our Lord's next phrase in John 17:3: 'that they may know you, the only true God ...'. By using the words 'true' and 'only', Jesus is clearly presenting God as over and against something else. It is obvious that He is cautioning us against idols and false gods. Both Jesus and John knew the tendency in all of us to have divided loyalties. Idols are an expression of a universal tendency – the tendency to put something in the place of God. Anything that becomes a centre of love and attention – a love and attention greater than the love and attention we give to God – is an idol. Idolatry is a substitution – the substitution of the lesser for the greater.

O God, help me to give myself to You, as You give Yourself to me – fully, wholly and entirely. In Christ's name I pray. Amen.

'Is your face towards me?'

FOR READING AND MEDITATION
HEBREWS 1:1–14

'The Son is the radiance of God's glory and the exact representation of his being …' (v.3)

The One who said the words 'the only true God' immediately went on to put Himself in the same position as God: 'the only true God, and Jesus Christ, whom you have sent'. An idol misrepresents God; Jesus represents Him. Is Jesus like God in status, character and life? Fully and truly like Him? I would respond with an unqualified 'Yes'. In Jesus we have a God with a face. 'Is your face towards me, Daddy?' said a little boy to his father, who had taken his son into his own bed because he was afraid of a midnight storm. 'Yes,' replied the father, 'it is.' The little boy then soon fell asleep. Jesus gives God a face, and that face is towards us – always.

O God my Father, I am so grateful that in Jesus I have a God with a face. And when I look into that face I see what You are like. Amen.

A secret of success

FOR READING AND MEDITATION
JOHN 19:28–37

*'When he had received the drink, Jesus said, "It is
finished."' (v.30)*

We consider now our Lord's words in verse 4 of
John 17: 'I have brought you glory on earth by
completing the work you gave me to do.' When Jesus
reviews His 33 years of ministry on earth, He gathers
it all up in one tremendous statement: 'It is finished.'
There were many things the disciples (and others)
wanted our Lord to do which He steadfastly resisted.
And He did so because His main concern was to follow
His Father's agenda, not the agenda of others. Is not this
the secret of true spiritual success? Our Lord glorified the
Father because He got His job description directly from
the Father's hand and not from the hands of others. So
must we.

*Father, help me learn this lesson – that I need to listen to
You to discover what You want me to do, and not to the
demands of others. Amen.*

Christ's *finished* work

FOR READING AND MEDITATION
JOHN 9:1–12

'As long as it is day, we must do the work of him who sent me.' (v.4)

The work our Lord came to do was the work of reconciliation – of bringing sinful but repentant men and women into relationship with a pardoning God. Four great facts define the gospel: 'a baby in a cradle, a man upon a cross, a body in a tomb, a King upon a throne'. Christ's mission involved an incarnation, a death by crucifixion, a resurrection, and a final triumphant ascent to the eternal throne. No one but Christ could accomplish this, and the beginning of Christian faith is the acceptance of these facts. The proof that we are Christians lies in our belief that Christ alone could effect the work of reconciliation with God; we rest upon that finished work.

Father, the work Your Son accomplished here on earth is the full and final payment for our salvation. May we rest on that finished work. Amen.

Homesick for heaven?

FOR READING AND MEDITATION
ISAIAH 42:1–13

'I am the LORD; that is my name! I will not give my glory to another ...' (v.8)

The next petition our Lord makes is this: 'And now, Father, glorify me in your presence with the glory I had with you before the world began' (John 17:5). No other person on earth could ever have spoken those words. As Isaiah reminds us in the words of today's text, God does not share His glory with another, meaning anyone less than Himself. Yet Jesus shared the Father's glory before the world was made, and recognised that it was properly His. Do we sense in the Saviour a homesickness for heaven? Perhaps so. I'm glad, though, that His desire to return to heaven was not as great as His determination to complete the work His Father had given Him to do. For that we owe Him an eternal debt of gratitude.

Lord Jesus Christ, You stayed here on earth and suffered agony on a cross so that I might one day join You in glory. 'All honour and praise be unto You for ever.' Amen.

No attitude problem

FOR READING AND MEDITATION
PHILIPPIANS 2:1–11

'Your attitude should be the same as that of Christ Jesus ...'
(v.5)

Our Lord's life here on earth was characterised by a continual self-emptying – a laying aside of glory. Ray C. Stedman says, 'It was not merely that which Jesus did which glorified the Father. It was His willingness to be always available, to be forever giving of Himself, that glorified God.' Jesus was great by what He did, but He was great also by the attitude with which He did it. Throughout His life He had a heart that was ready to obey, an ear that was ready to hear, and a will that was ready to be subject to the Father. Does the same attitude lie behind all that we do for God? If not, then however much we accomplish in terms of quantity, it will be of little worth.

Father, please help me to grasp the truth that my attitude determines my spiritual altitude. May I aim to be as self-giving as Jesus. Amen.

'The best photograph of God'

FOR READING AND MEDITATION
JOHN 1:1–18

'No-one has ever seen God, but God the One and Only, who is at the Father's side, has made him known.' (v.18)

Why was it necessary for Jesus to reveal God to us? Without Jesus we would never have known what God is like – really like. Our misconceptions would have kept us away from Him. All the other ways in which God has revealed Himself – nature, words, and so on – are somewhat limited. They reveal God, but not completely. However, when I look up to God through Jesus I know what God is like – perfectly. Jesus reveals in personal form the character of God, His righteousness and His wonderful saving love. A little boy in Sunday school who, when asked what he thought about Jesus, replied, 'Jesus is the best photograph God ever had taken.' He is.

Father, I need not wonder if You are like Jesus, or Jesus is like You, for You are one in nature and one in purpose. Amen.

Out of the world

FOR READING AND MEDITATION
JOHN 15:18–27

'... you do not belong to the world, but I have chosen you out of the world.' (v.19)

Our Lord's prayer continues with these words: 'I have revealed you to those whom you gave me out of the world' (John 17:6). What does this say to us? The first thing it says is that a follower of Christ is a person who does not belong to this world. We have tended (especially here in the West) to divide society horizontally into three classes: lower class, middle class and upper class. It is fair to say that nowadays these classes are being broken down, but in many minds they still exist. God, however, does not divide humanity horizontally but perpendicularly. On one side are those who are of the world and on the other those who are of Christ.

Father, You have taken me out of the world; please take the world's attitudes out of me. In Jesus' name I ask it. Amen.

Obeying the Word

FOR READING AND MEDITATION
I JOHN 2:1–17

'We know that we have come to know him if we obey his commands.' (v.3)

W e focus now on the words, 'They were yours; you gave them to me and they have obeyed your word.' Another characteristic of a Christian is that he or she is someone who receives God's Word and keeps it. To 'obey the Word' does not mean we will never have times of doubt and struggle, but that we hold on to it nevertheless. The disciples could not always understand the Master, but they did stay with Him for three and a half years. Jesus' true disciples realise that nothing matters in this world more than the truth of God, and even in the midst of their struggles they allow themselves to be controlled by that truth. He keeps us and we keep His Word.

Lord Jesus Christ, although I do not always understand I commit myself to always obey. Amen.

A day for decision

FOR READING AND MEDITATION
MATTHEW 16:13–20

'Who do you say I am?' … 'You are the Christ, the Son of the living God.' (vv.15–16)

We must be clear as to who Jesus is. No one can claim to be a Christian unless they are convinced that Jesus is the Son of God. We fool ourselves when we look at people who live good moral lives and, on that basis alone, categorise them as Christians. Good, upright, moral living is required of every Christian, but that does not make a person one of Christ's disciples. The first mark of a Christian is a clear understanding of the Person of Christ – who He is and why He came. If you believe this and are willing to receive Christ into your heart as your Saviour and Lord then bow your head now and pray this prayer:

O God my Father, I come to You through Christ Your Son. I believe that He was sent from heaven to be my Saviour and I receive Him now into my heart by faith. Make me a true Christian. Amen.

A long prayer session!

'... he is able to save completely those who come to God through him, because he always lives to intercede for them.' (v.25)

Marvellous though it was that our Lord prayed for His disciples in John 17, the passage before us today tells us something even more thrilling – that now in heaven He is interceding for us. Just think of it: at this very moment our Lord sits on the throne interceding for you and for me. If we let this thought occupy us more than it does at present, it would, I am sure, make a tremendous difference to the way we face our days. Christ has been engaged in this task of praying for His people since He returned to heaven 2,000 years ago. That makes it the longest prayer session in history!

Father, how humbled and awed I am by the knowledge that Jesus, Your Son and my Advocate, intercedes for me before Your eternal throne. Amen.

'I'm praying for you!'

FOR READING AND MEDITATION
LUKE 22:24–38

'Simon, Simon, Satan has asked to sift you as wheat.' (v.31)

Christ prayed for the disciples during their hour of bewilderment and what is even more thrilling is that He is interceding now for us before the royal throne. Did you notice that in our text for today Jesus mentions Simon's name twice? It would have been the same when our Lord was praying for him, I imagine; his name would have been often on the Saviour's lips. Are you feeling battered and beaten by the adverse circumstances of your life at this moment? Do you wonder where your next ounce of strength is coming from? Then be transformed by this thought: your Saviour is interceding for you on the throne. He is praying for you. And by name!

Lord Jesus Christ, my Advocate and my great High Priest, please take this truth and burn it into my spirit until it transforms me. Amen.

A little means a lot

FOR READING AND MEDITATION
JOHN 15:1–16

'You did not choose me, but I chose you and appointed you to go and bear fruit – fruit that will last.' (v.16)

Jesus prays, 'And glory has come to me through them' (John 17:10). Our Lord said many things about His disciples, but this is probably the most staggering thing of all. An observer watching the disciples over a period of time might have concluded that they were quarrelsome, jealous, dull and blundering, and seen nothing more. But Jesus perceived that deep down in their hearts they were definitely committed to Him, and had already brought Him glory by their obedient trust. Compared to what it might have been, their commitment was perhaps little. But to Jesus the little meant a lot. His gaze penetrates our flaws, frailties and deficiencies. He sees right into our hearts – and knows what is true of us.

Lord Jesus Christ, may the love and commitment that is in my heart bring glory to You also. Amen.

Who cares?

FOR READING AND MEDITATION
MATTHEW 6:25–34

'If … God clothes the grass of the field … will he not much more clothe you, O you of little faith?' (v.30)

The focus of Christ's petition in John 17:11 is found in the two words 'protect them'. There were many other things Christ could have prayed for at this moment in the life of His disciples. He could have prayed 'use them', 'teach them', or 'guide them'. But as He is about to leave them to go to the cross He puts into one brief phrase His heart's greatest desire – that they might be divinely kept and divinely protected. How this highlights once again the love and concern our Lord has for His people. He prays for them even when His death is imminent. Oh, if only we could fully grasp this fact – that our Lord's concern for us is greater than the concern we have for ourselves.

O Jesus, let the truth of Your concern for me be more than mere theory. Let it grip me, impact me – even stagger me. Amen.

The knowledge of God

FOR READING AND MEDITATION
HEBREWS 2:10–18

'I will declare your name to my brothers; in the presence of the congregation I will sing your praises.' (v.12)

Our Lord's first petition for His disciples was that they might be protected and kept, 'by the power of your name' (John 17:11). Names in the Bible are more than mere designations; they are definitions. A name in Scripture does more than identify someone; it tells us what kind of person they are – their character, their essential nature. The name reveals the person. In the Old Testament God revealed His nature to us through many different names. The Old Testament saints knew Him as *El Elyon* (God Most High, Gen. 14:18), *El Shaddai* (The Nourisher of His People, Gen. 17:1), *Jehovah Jireh* (the LORD Provides, Gen. 22:14) and so on. In the New Testament there is no greater name than Jesus – *Saviour*.

Father, I realise that if Jesus had not come I could never have known You as You really are – my Saviour and my friend. Amen.

One name, one way

FOR READING AND MEDITATION
GENESIS 32:22–32

'Jacob said, "Please tell me your name."' (v.29)

J acob realised that once he knew the man's name he
would have a clearer understanding of the nature of the
one before him. Similarly, our greatest need is to know
the name of God, for when we know His name we know
Him and can come to an intimate understanding of Him.
The Father, as the Bible makes clear in so many different
places, sent Jesus into the world to declare His name,
to unfold His character, to reveal His essential nature.
In praying that the disciples might be protected by the
power of God's name, Jesus is asking that they might be
kept in that knowledge and in that understanding; that
they might be protected by the special awareness they
had of God as revealed through Him and only Him.

*Father, how grateful I am that in Jesus You offer me Your
all. All honour and glory be to His most glorious name.
Amen.*

Jesus *is* God

FOR READING AND MEDITATION
JOHN 10:22–42

'I and the Father are one.' (v.30)

Christ is praying here that the same unity which exists between Him and His Father might be experienced by His disciples. The men who actually heard those words understood Jesus to be claiming equality with God and picked up stones to stone Him. What a staggering thought it is that the carpenter of Nazareth is one with the Father – God in human form. I remember being struck by this thought during the first weeks of my conversion. I could not get over it then, and I have not been able to get over it since. Be staggered by this truth if you will, but never let go of it. Jesus Christ is God. Not like God, but fully God. He is God in human form.

My Father, I rejoice that because Jesus is both God and man He provides a safe access from here to eternity. Thank You, my Father. Amen.

We are kept

FOR READING AND MEDITATION
1 CORINTHIANS 1:1–9

'He will keep you strong to the end, so that you will be blameless on the day of our Lord Jesus Christ.' (v.8)

L et us focus on the words of our Lord in John 17:12: 'While I was with them, I protected them and kept them safe by that name you gave me.' It is impossible to read these words without again sensing the Saviour's intense concern and care for His disciples. If we spent more time focusing on how great is our Lord's concern for us, and understood all the implications of this, we would suffer less anxiety and be less frenzied and less flurried. The thought in the mind of our Lord as he utters these words is: 'Father while I was with them I kept them in the knowledge and worship of You. Now that I am going away, I am handing that task over to You.'

Lord Jesus Christ, I dread to think where I might be today were it not for Your wondrous keeping power. Amen.

He keeps us safe

FOR READING AND MEDITATION
I PETER 2:13–25

'… now you have returned to the Shepherd and Overseer of your souls.' (v.25)

We saw yesterday that Jesus says He protected and kept the disciples while He was with them, but how did He? One way was by His personal petitions on their behalf. Another way was by His frequent warnings and cautions. Jesus kept the disciples also by His teaching. He taught them about the world and its subtlety, about sin and its enticements, about the devil and his blandishments. And the way He kept them is the way He keeps us – the only difference being that through the power and presence of the Holy Spirit He can be with each one of us not just some of the time but all of the time.

Lord Jesus Christ, thank You that through the Holy Spirit You confront me, uphold me and comfort me. Whatever I am it is all because of You. Amen.

My joy

FOR READING AND MEDITATION
JOHN 16:17–24

'Ask and you will receive, and your joy will be complete.'
(v.24)

The next verse we focus on as we move through our Lord's prayer in John 17 is this: 'I am coming to you now, but I say these things while I am still in the world, so that they may have the full measure of my joy within them' (v.13). 'My joy.' In the hours immediately before His death the Saviour wants His disciples to be partakers of His own deep joy. Jesus spoke about joy a number of times in His teachings, and it was a key element in the section of His final discourses to His disciples recorded in John 15 and 16. It appears frequently in the epistles too. I do not believe I am going too far when I say that joy is a major theme of the New Testament.

Father, however much joy I have I still ask for more. Fill me with joy and fill me to overflowing. In Jesus' name. Amen.

His joyous soul

FOR READING AND MEDITATION
JOHN 15:1–11

'... so that my joy may be in you and that your joy may be complete.' (v.11)

Some think that joy is a matter of temperament – whatever they mean by that. The Greeks had a theory that we are all born with a certain cast of mind and that this remains practically unmodified throughout the whole of a person's life. There may be some truth in this, but the joy that Jesus gives has nothing to do with our disposition. It comes directly from His joyous soul. 'My joy,' He says. Joy is not self-generated – we cannot reach down into the depths of our being and pump it up. Christ possesses joy in all its fullness, and when we live in Him then we possess it also because He gives it to us. It is as simple as that. Permit me to ask this personal question: Are you a joyful person?

O Father, in this sad and gloomy world please help me to spread the Saviour's everlasting joy. In Jesus' name I ask it. Amen.

A little bit of heaven!

FOR READING AND MEDITATION
HABAKKUK 3:1–19

'... I will rejoice in the LORD, I will be joyful in God my Saviour.' (v.18)

U nless we are careful and get the balance right we can overlook the fact that it is possible for us to enjoy something of heaven while we are here on planet Earth. We can have a little bit of heaven to go to heaven in. I am convinced that there is more available here – more joy, peace and happiness – than many believers actually experience. Becoming a Christian is a serious business, but once we are Christians we become inheritors of a deep and lasting joy. Jesus was a serious man yet He was a joyful man also. Take Jesus seriously and you too will have access to an unfathomable joy. Christ's joy is your joy; it is your unassailable birthright.

Father, I see that Your joy is my birthright. Please fill me with joy and help me to spread it wherever I go. In Jesus' name. Amen.

Hated by the world

FOR READING AND MEDITATION
ROMANS 12:1–8

'Do not conform any longer to the pattern of this world, but be transformed by the renewing of your mind.' (v.2)

In John 17 Jesus prays: 'I have given them your word and the world has hated them, for they are not of the world any more than I am of the world' (v.14). We must not fail to recognise that once we come over on to the side of Christ the world will hate us. Should we then go out of our way to court opposition, to deliberately set out to antagonise people so that they might persecute us? No, for love of persecution reveals an unhealthy personality; it is masochism. The world did not hate Jesus because He was deliberately antagonistic. It hated Him because of His sheer purity and holiness. It must be the same with us also.

Father, do Your people reflect so little of Your purity and holiness that the world does not notice us? If so, forgive us. Make us more like You. Amen.

Why are we not more hated?

FOR READING AND MEDITATION
I JOHN 3:11–24

'Do not be surprised, my brothers, if the world hates you.'
(v.13)

M any years ago I used to wonder why the men and
women of the world do not hate the non Christians
who are ethical and moral but they hate those who
truly live the Christian life. The ultimate problem with
the human heart, we must remember, is that of pride,
and this is why moral people are the ones who so often
hate Christ most of all. Self-centred moral people who
rest on their own laurels hate Christ because they sense
that He is going to condemn their prideful self-effort and
call them to trust in Him. When they see a Christian
drawing on Christ for their life, and depending on Him
to make their life work, they end up hating that Christian
just as much as they hate Christ.

O God, help me to be more like Jesus and less like the world.
In His name I ask it. Amen.

Guarded!

FOR READING AND MEDITATION
2 TIMOTHY 1:1–18

'... I know whom I have believed, and am convinced that he is able to guard what I have entrusted to him ...' (v.12)

The next petition we come to in our Lord's prayer is this: 'My prayer is not that you take them out of the world but that you protect them from the evil one' (John 17:15). There are many reasons why Christians are to remain here on earth. If believers were taken from the world to heaven as soon as they were saved who would preach the gospel? Who would represent Christ's cause? And who would act as salt and light in the world? Christ knew better than anyone the evil that is in the world, and He knew also the weaknesses of His disciples. But He was aware of the keeping power of His heavenly Father, and His confidence was in that.

O God, may I never forget that my arrival in heaven will not be a testimony to my self-sufficiency, but to divine sufficiency. Amen.

Influence or intelligence?

FOR READING AND MEDITATION
I PETER 5:1–14

'Your enemy the devil prowls around like a roaring lion looking for someone to devour.' (v.8)

The last phrase of John 17:15 is: '… protect them from the evil one.' Our Lord knew that His disciples faced not only an evil influence but an evil intelligence. Oswald Chambers said, 'The root of sin is the belief that God is not good.' This was the devil's chief weapon in Eden, and it still is. It was doubt concerning God's goodness that led to the first sin. Doubt is not an evil in itself, but when it is allowed to linger and not firmly ejected, it can soon lead to a loss of confidence in God. Though you may occasionally doubt the goodness of God, bring those doubts to the place where God's goodness has been most clearly validated – the cross. A God who loved us enough to die for us has just got to be good.

O God, I am so grateful for the cross. It proves Your love in a way that lies beyond all doubt. I simply bring my doubts to Calvary. Amen.

A change of citizenship

FOR READING AND MEDITATION
PHILIPPIANS 3:1–21

'But our citizenship is in heaven. And we eagerly await a Saviour from there, the Lord Jesus Christ ...' (v.20)

John 17:16 reads: 'They are not of the world, even as I am not of it.' The disciples may well have displayed worldly attitudes from time to time. Nevertheless, because of their relationship with Christ, they had experienced a change of citizenship. Just as Christ belonged to the eternal kingdom, so did they. Because of their allegiance to Him they had been given a new passport, so to speak, that brought them under a new authority and into a new culture and a new kingdom. Of course they still displayed some of the characteristics of the old culture – but that does not mean they belonged to it. There's a big difference between losing your way and losing your address.

Gracious Father, I am so thankful that I am a citizen of heaven – a new country with a new culture. Amen.

Changed from the inside

FOR READING AND MEDITATION
1 THESSALONIANS 4:1–18

'It is God's will that you should be sanctified ...' (v.3)

What does our Lord mean when he prays for His disciples to be 'sanctified'? The word 'sanctify' has a variety of meanings in Scripture but basically it means two things: first, to be set apart for God's use, and second, to be made fit for God's use. The primary meaning of this word always has two aspects – dedication and purification. We begin to see more clearly why our Lord prayed that His disciples should not be taken out of the world. He had in mind something better: that the world should be taken out of them. We can't stop the world being outside us, but we can stop it being inside us. Christ wants us to be changed not from the outside in but from the inside out.

Father, help me understand that sanctification basically results from a relationship. The more I get to know You the more I become like You. Amen.

The power of God's truth

FOR READING AND MEDITATION
PSALM 119:1–16

'How can a young man keep his way pure? By living according to your word.' (v.9)

S anctification is being set apart *from* the world and being set apart *to* God and there are two main ways in which God sanctifies us: through the Holy Spirit and through the Word of God – what Jesus describes in His prayer as 'the truth'. As we meditate on the Bible, God, by the power of the Holy Spirit, opens our understanding of it and enables us to comprehend it. Whatever great experiences God may give us through the power of the Holy Spirit, we must never use them as a substitute for taking the truths that He shows us in His Word and applying them to our lives day by day and moment by moment. I need both the knowledge of the Word and the continuous flow of the Spirit to develop and grow.

Father, help me understand Your Word, for I see that it is there, under the Spirit's guidance, that I find the power to change, develop and grow. Amen.

What are we to believe?

FOR READING AND MEDITATION
1 PETER 3:8–22

'But in your hearts set apart Christ as Lord.' (v.15)

The theory of sanctification is not difficult to understand – believing and accepting the Word of truth to produce change – but the application of it seems to give many Christians great difficulty. We are too accustomed to believing our feelings rather than God's Word. When, as a young man, I shared this problem with my pastor, this was his reply: 'Yes, it takes time to overcome that kind of problem; just make sure it does not take you longer than it ought to.' Over the years, whenever my feelings have contradicted the Word, I have learned to say, 'God, it's my feelings I need to disbelieve, not Your Word. What I see in Your Word is fact. Inevitably so.'

Father, help me to trust Your Word, even when my senses may be screaming otherwise. In Jesus' name. Amen.

The big picture

FOR READING AND MEDITATION
EPHESIANS 3:1–21

*'And I pray that you ... may have power ... to grasp how
wide and long and high and deep is the love of Christ ...'*
(vv.17–18)

M uch will be said about the crucifixion during the
Easter season in churches but let me help you see
what I call 'the big picture'. Before the creation of the
world, God decided to have a people for Himself who
would be His joy through time and eternity. Once He
had marked out those who were to be His, He gave
them to Christ, so that the Son might make them a
people fit for His special possession and enjoyment. See
the big picture. Jesus died not just so that we could
have our sins forgiven but so that He could live His life
in us and through us. Can anything be more awesome,
more wonderful, than to know that Christ and the Holy
Spirit are at work within us with the purpose of bringing
God pleasure?

*O God, the fact that I am one who can bring You pleasure
is almost too awesome to contemplate. Help me not just to
accept it but rejoice in it. Amen.*

Forsaken by all

'Then all the disciples deserted him and fled.' (v.56)

I believe Christ knew His disciples would forsake Him, but He knew also that despite their fear, their hesitancy, their denials and their doubts, deep down in their hearts they would want to believe that what He had said about coming back from the dead would happen. The reason why I think that is because I am aware that the same thing occurs whenever I am in a crisis. I want to believe what God says even though things look dark all around. Often I have found myself wishing the desire to have faith in Him was stronger, but I have rejoiced many times in my life that however weak it is, the conviction always remains that God will be true to His Word. It's part, I think, of being His child.

O God, how thankful I am that doubts are temporary but faith is permanent. All honour and glory be to Your name. Amen.

New life for everyone!

FOR READING AND MEDITATION
MATTHEW 28:1–15

'He is not here; he has risen, just as he said.' (v.6)

Dr W.E. Sangster, the famous Methodist, after being weakened by a disease which progressively atrophied his muscles, found himself one Easter Sunday morning without the ability to use his voice. He wrote a note to his family that said this: 'It is sad to wake up on Easter morning and have no voice with which to shout, "He is risen!" But it would be sadder still to have a voice, and not want to shout it.' The new life that came out of that tomb is now resident in you and in me. If that is not a reason for shouting 'He is risen!' at the top of one's voice then I don't know what is.

O God, I feel like echoing the words of the angel and shouting them from the roof tops: 'He is not here; he has risen!' Amen.

The divine equation

FOR READING AND MEDITATION
JOHN 20:1–23

'As the Father has sent me, I am sending you.' (v.21)

We now consider the next statement in John 17: 'As you sent me into the world, I have sent them into the world' (John 17:18). This is what I like to call 'the divine equation'. As – So. In an equation one side has to balance the other. Christ has fulfilled His side of the equation – and now the disciples are expected to fulfil theirs. We who are Christ's disciles in the twenty-first century must never forget that the only way people in the world can learn of Christ is from what we show them and what we tell them – first by our lives, then by our lips. Every Christian is to be an evangelist.

Lord Jesus, if we fail to let the world know of the Father then He will remain unknown. Please help us, dear Lord. We dare not fail. Amen.

True dedication

FOR READING AND MEDITATION
HEBREWS 10:1–18

'Here I am ... I have come to do your will, O God.' (v.7)

'For them I sanctify myself,' says the Master, 'that they too may be truly sanctified' (John 17:19). What Jesus is doing here is using the word 'sanctify' in its primary sense of dedication, not purification. He had set Himself apart for the special task which had been given Him by the Father, and was continuing in that task with a deep and joyful commitment. He was consecrating every part of Him. His whole personality, everything He was as God and man, all His powers and attributes, were dedicated to the task of bringing glory to God. The Son of God devoted Himself utterly to the work of redemption, and gave Himself to the task of setting us free from sin with unswerving selflessness. What a Saviour!

O God, help us exclude everything that does not contribute to Your purposes, and serve You with unswerving devotion. Amen.

Saved to serve!

FOR READING AND MEDITATION
MATTHEW 28:16–20

'Therefore go and make disciples of all nations …' (v.19)

Jesus prays for the disciples and 'their message' in John 17:20. Some preachers use this illustration: soon after the resurrection, when Christ had returned to heaven, the angels gathered around Him and enquired, 'Master, what plans do You have for ensuring that Your gospel will be preached throughout the world?' The Lord explained that He had left the task completely in the hands of His followers. The angels seemed surprised at this, and one of them said, 'But Master, Your disciples are so fickle and unreliable. What if they fail? What other arrangements have You made?' Solemnly the Lord looked at them and answered, 'None. This is the only way My gospel can be made known. I have no other plan!'

Father, nothing could be clearer – we are not saved merely to be safe but saved to make others safe. We are saved to serve! Amen.

APRIL 20

Our model for unity

FOR READING AND MEDITATION
PSALM 133:1–3

'How good and pleasant it is when brothers live together in unity!' (v.1)

Our Lord now asks that the same unity which exists between Him and His Father might be found also among all His followers (John 20:21). Unity is often confused with similar-sounding words such as union, uniformity and unanimity. Unity is this: the bonding of one believer to another because of an overriding sense of belonging to the same family – a disposition of oneness that is so deeply ingrained it brings its influence to bear on all thinking, all decisions and all actions. We are going much deeper than denominational affiliation now; we are talking about the kind of unity that the Son has with the Father. That is the type of unity which should characterise relationships in the Church.

Lord Jesus, the unity You have with Your Father is the kind of unity we crave. Help us achieve that unity – and quickly. Amen.

Why ecumenism fails

FOR READING AND MEDITATION
ROMANS 15:1–13

'May the God who gives endurance and encouragement give you a spirit of unity among yourselves as you follow Christ Jesus ...' (v.5)

Unity is not something that can be imposed upon the Church by simply getting together; unity is something that has to be exposed from within the Body of Christ by those who know without any shadow of doubt that they belong to Him. The first unity to get straight, then, is our unity with God. One of the main difficulties in the Church of today is that we are trying to relate to one another without considering our relationship with God. When Peter was rightly related to God, 'he stood up with the Eleven' (Acts 2:14). Previously the disciples had been at variance and he had stood against them (Luke 22:24). Unity with God made the difference.

Loving heavenly Father, may Your people be so one with You that they will become one with each other. Amen.

Spiritual unity

FOR READING AND MEDITATION
EPHESIANS 4:1–16

'… so that the body of Christ may be built up until we all reach unity in the faith …' (vv.12–13)

The unity being spoken about here is a spiritual unity – the kind of unity our Lord was thinking of in His prayer in John 17. The moment we enter the Church we become part of a Body that is united by the power and energy of the Holy Spirit. Our task then is not to 'make' unity, but simply to maintain it. It is a unity of people who have become spiritual – who are born again. We belong to Christ and we realise that because of this we belong to everyone else who belongs to Christ. A world of difference exists between this kind of internal unity and the external unity so often spoken of in Christian circles.

O God, forgive us that often we are more eager to discover a person's denomination than we are to rejoice that they are our brother or sister. Amen.

Effective evangelism

FOR READING AND MEDITATION
2 CHRONICLES 30:1–20

'... in Judah the hand of God was on the people to give them unity of mind ...' (v.12)

The more we give ourselves to the Trinity the easier it will be to give ourselves to our brothers and sisters. There is one thing more our Lord prays – something I think you must admit is quite staggering: 'that the world may believe that you have sent me'. It is the unity of believers, our Lord says, that will convince men and women of His mission to this world. The visible unity of believers is, then, the greatest form of evangelism. What a rebuke this is to the groundless and often bitter divisions among Christians. How wonderful it is to see believers united, not so much within their denominations, but in Christ. And how sad it is when that unity is not present.

O God, how we hinder the work of evangelism by our fragmentation. Forgive us, renew us and unite us. In Jesus' name we pray. Amen.

The glory 'given'

FOR READING AND MEDITATION
HEBREWS 2:1–9

'But we see Jesus … now crowned with glory and honour because he suffered death …' (v.9)

There is a great deal of debate among Bible teachers as to the glory Jesus is talking about in John 17:22. My own view is that our Lord is anticipating the glory He would receive in heaven and which, in turn, He would share with all His people. This is the glory that we read about in our passage for today. When Christ returned to heaven He did not leave His humanity behind Him, and thus He is now glorified and sits on the throne not only as God but as the God Man. This, I believe, is the special glory He speaks of in John 17:24 – the glory given to Him by His Father because of what He has accomplished for you and for me.

O Saviour, what joy it gives me to know that my humanity is represented on the eternal throne. All honour and glory be to Your name. Amen.

Two indwellings

FOR READING AND MEDITATION
JOHN 3:1–21

'For God did not send his Son into the world to condemn the world, but to save the world through him.' (v.17)

In John 17:23 Jesus prays, 'I in them and you in me. May they be brought to complete unity to let the world know that you sent me and have loved them even as you have loved me.' There are two indwellings spoken of here: 'I in them and you in me.' The first is the dwelling of the Son in His followers, and the second is the dwelling of the Father in the Son. It is only because of the latter – the dwelling of the Father in the Son – that the former can take place – the dwelling of the Son in His followers. This, then, is the only formula for unity amongst Christ's followers.

Father, renew us and refresh us, that we might be the people You want us to be. In Jesus' name we ask it. Amen.

United in love

FOR READING AND MEDITATION
COLOSSIANS 2:1–23

'My purpose is that they may be encouraged in heart and united in love …' (v.2)

L et us reflect on the words 'you … have loved them even as you have loved me' (John 17:23) and recognise that God loves us in the way He loves Jesus. People in the world need to see that we are sustained by that love, empowered by that love and united by that love. This is what will impress them and be a witness to them. The more we are seen by the world to be dependent rather than independent, the more it will be affected by the gospel. Nothing can be of greater importance than this. This is the unity – the complete unity – that will shake the world.

O God, save us from living independently of You and each other. Unite us so that we might be a powerful witness to the world. Amen.

Our Lord's last will

FOR READING AND MEDITATION
JOHN 12:20–36

'Whoever serves me must follow me; and where I am, my servant also will be.' (v.26)

In John 17:24 we come to the verse which has been described as 'Christ's last will and testament'. Jesus' will for us in this verse is that we might be with Him and see His glory. To be included in someone's will is always wonderful because it reminds us that the person concerned held us in high regard and cared for us. But to be included in Christ's will stretches credulity. Yet it is true. It is His will that we be with Him in eternity and behold and participate in His glory. And nothing, absolutely nothing, can stop the Saviour's last will and testament being executed in the manner He desires. Hallelujah!

O Father, what a prospect: one day I am going to see Jesus in all His glory! Even so, come Lord Jesus! Amen.

We know

FOR READING AND MEDITATION
JOHN 16:25–33

'… the Father himself loves you because you have loved me and have believed that I came from God.' (v.27)

The Lord's main concern in John 17:25 is not for the world but for His chosen people: 'they know that you have sent me.' These words must not be taken to mean that Christ has no love or concern for those who will not come to Him. God loves all His creation, but He has a special love for those who come to know Him through Christ. We who are His children must not gloat over this fact, but we can glory in it. We can be sure we are Christ's when we are able to look into the face of the Father and say, 'We know that You have sent Him into the world.' We *know*.

Father, no knowledge rejoices my heart more than the knowledge that You sent Your Son to be my Saviour. Thank You, my Father. Amen.

Near is not enough

FOR READING AND MEDITATION
COLOSSIANS 1:15–29

'… God has chosen to make known … the glorious riches
of this mystery, which is Christ in you, the hope of glory.'
(v.27)

In John 17:26 Christ says that not only has He made
the Father known but that He will continue to make
Him known. Our Lord is just about to go to the cross yet
His thought is not of Himself but of continuing in the
task which God had given Him – to reveal the Father's
heart to the world. Jesus closes His prayer with these
words: 'that I myself may be in them'. William Law
commented, 'A Christ not in us is a Christ not ours.'
This, in a sense, is what Paul is declaring in our text for
today. We must have Christ within. Christ *near* is not
enough. Christ *above* is not enough. Christ *outside* of us
is not enough. Only Christ *within* is enough.

*O Father, it is no exaggeration to describe the words 'Christ
in me' as the essence of the gospel, for I see that a Christ not
in me is a Christ not mine. Amen.*

A final summary

FOR READING AND MEDITATION
JOHN 17:1–26

'My prayer is not for them alone. I pray also for those who will believe in me through their message ...' (v.20)

Three things in particular stand out from our studies of John 17. First, the fact that as Christians we are God's *chosen* people. Long before time began, the Trinity met in a kind of Divine Council. Here the Father looked into the future and saw those destined for salvation and marked them as His. God's next step was to give them to His Son so that He might wash them, sanctify them and bring them into intimate fellowship with the Trinity. Second, the realisation that on the eve of His agonising death on the cross, our Saviour's foremost thoughts were not for Himself but for those whom His Father had given Him. Third, the awareness that the more we allow the truths contained in this chapter to take hold of us, the less we will fall prey to anxiety and uncertainty.

O God my Father, thank You for what I have learned from this my Saviour's most wonderful prayer. Burn its truths deep into my soul. In Jesus' name. Amen.

Back to the future

FOR READING AND MEDITATION
EPHESIANS 3:1–13

'His intent was that now, through the church, the manifold wisdom of God should be made known ...' (v.10)

We begin a series of meditations on the characteristics of the Christian Church based on the Church of the first century. After one Billy Graham crusade some liberal ministers complained, 'Billy Graham has set the Church in Los Angeles back 100 years.' When Billy heard this he commented, 'Oh dear, I am so sorry ... I was really trying to set it back 2,000 years!' It is my conviction that every local church would do well to study the Acts of the Apostles with a view to identifying how far we have drifted from first principles. One thing is sure: if the Church of the twenty-first century does not match the Church of the first century then there is not much hope for the future.

Father, open our eyes that we may see where we, Your people, have drifted from Your purposes. And begin with me I pray. Amen.

The Great Contemporary

FOR READING AND MEDITATION
ACTS 1:1–5

'In my former book, Theophilus, I wrote about all that Jesus began to do and to teach ...' (v.1)

One word in the opening sentence tells us what the book of Acts is all about. That word is 'began'. What Jesus began in the Gospels is continued in Acts. The Saviour had not finished when He ascended on high and returned to the royal throne. Through the Holy Spirit, He continues ministering in the lives of those committed to Him. It is the risen Christ we see at work in the Acts of the Apostles, moving in the hearts of men and women and bringing them into His Church. The ministry of Jesus may have had a beginning, but it will never have an ending. Someone has written of Jesus, 'You can never catch up with Him as He is always on before – the Great Contemporary'.

O Jesus, I am so thankful that the ministry You began when You came to this earth continues still. Amen.

The glorious Ascension

FOR READING AND MEDITATION
ACTS 1:6–11

'... he was taken up before their very eyes, and a cloud hid him from their sight.' (v.9)

Ian Macpherson says that the New Testament represents the Ascension as a sublime drama in three acts: secession, procession and accession. By secession he means the withdrawal of Christ from the earth. Our Lord not only had to leave the earth, He had to be seen to leave it. The Ascension, however, involved not only a secession but also a procession: 'When he ascended on high, he led captives in his train and gave gifts to men' (Eph. 4:8). Our Lord had behind Him a train of vanquished foes – probably the spiritual enemies who were defeated at the cross. Finally, accession. Our Lord ascended to a throne and sits there now at the right hand of God – King of kings and Lord of lords. Hallelujah!

Risen, exalted and glorified Lord, You went from the here to the everywhere – out of our sight, but nearer to our hearts. Amen.

A ten-day prayer meeting

FOR READING AND MEDITATION
ACTS 1:12–26

'They all joined together constantly in prayer ...' (v.14)

The apostles, together with over 100 of Christ's followers, 'joined together constantly in prayer'. We in the Christian Church tend to make much of the Day of Pentecost (and rightly so), but often we overlook what happened in the ten days between the Ascension and Pentecost. This, remember, was the first time the believers had met together after their Lord had returned to heaven – and they met together to pray. Mary the mother of Jesus was there, we are told (v.14). Isn't it interesting that the last glimpse we have of the mother of our Lord is at a prayer meeting! She who had carried the Saviour in her womb – her gift to the world – was now waiting to be filled with the Spirit – Christ's gift to her.

Father, I know that all great movements begin in prayer. Help us to pray more earnestly, dear Father. In Jesus' name. Amen.

Why a Church at all?

FOR READING AND MEDITATION
MATTHEW 16:13–20

'... on this rock I will build my church, and the gates of Hades will not overcome it.' (v.18)

Why is there a Church at all? Because Christ founded it. He said, 'On this rock I will build my church.' The Church was not the idea or invention of the disciples. It was founded by Christ and is therefore a divine institution. One of the chief reasons for the Church being on earth is to continue the work which Christ began. Acts shows us that what Christ once did, the Church was now doing. In terms of increase and the number of miracles that were performed, greater things happened through Christ in His Church than through Christ in the flesh. Never forget it was Christ in His Church that turned the Ancient World upside down (Acts 17:6, AV)!

Father, You long for Your Church to be bold, adventurous and victorious. Revive us again and set us on fire for You. Amen.

'They're drunk!'

FOR READING AND MEDITATION
ACTS 2:1–13

'Some … made fun of them and said, "They have had too much wine."' (v.13)

The first of the distinctives of the Early Church is this: *the energising ministry of the Holy Spirit.* The Day of Pentecost is one of the greatest days in the history of the Church. The two main accusations which were directed at the early Christians – 'They're drunk' and 'They're mad' – are rarely heard today. Most modern-day Christians do not come under this dark suspicion, though that is hardly to our credit. What would happen if we opened ourselves up to the Spirit as eagerly and responsively as did the Early Church? People would say the same about us as they said about the first believers: they're drunk and they're mad. Maybe the fact that they don't ought to be a matter of the greatest concern.

O God, forgive us if we lack exuberance and excitement in our Christian walk. Refresh us by Your Spirit and help us to show Your life to others. Amen.

The true euphoria

FOR READING AND MEDITATION
ACTS 2:14–21

'These men are not drunk, as you suppose.' (v.15)

Alcohol gives a person a spurious euphoria. It picks you up but then lets you down. The Holy Spirit gives a true euphoria. He picks you up without letting you down. Permit me to ask you two personal questions: Does your contact with the Holy Spirit produce in you feelings of exuberance, exhilaration and infectious joy? Has anyone ever decided that because of your commitment to Christ you are mad or you are drunk? Don't let anyone tell you that devotion and exuberance cannot go together. They can. It's one thing to have the Holy Spirit; it's another thing for the Holy Spirit to have us! Then, one sermon, anointed by the Spirit, resulted in 3,000 people being saved, now, as has been said, it may take 3,000 sermons to see one person saved!

O God, I long to be alive to You, intoxicated by You, filled with You. Please grant it, my Father. In Jesus' name. Amen.

3,000 resurrections!

FOR READING AND MEDITATION
ACTS 2:22–41

'When the people heard this, they were cut to the heart and said … "Brothers, what shall we do?"' (v.37)

The scene we are observing in the second chapter of Acts is so different from that which we see in our churches today. We are accustomed to hearing evangelists call people to be saved, but here the people are calling out to the evangelist, 'What must we do to be saved?' Such is the power of the Holy Spirit's conviction, that they are 'cut to the heart'. Oh, how desperately we need that same kind of energy flowing through the Church today. At Pentecost the same power that raised Christ from the dead – the Holy Spirit – raised 3,000 from the dead – 3,000 sinners who were dead in trespasses and sins!

Father, thank You that the Holy Spirit is available to us in just the same way that He was to the Early Church. Amen.

An ideal Christian meeting

FOR READING AND MEDITATION
ACTS 10:9–48

'… these people … have received the Holy Spirit just as we have.' (v.47)

When Peter arrives at the house of Cornelius, he finds himself in what has been described as an 'ideal Christian meeting'. It had an ideal chairman. Cornelius gave the kind of introduction every preacher would like to have: 'Now we are all here in the presence of God to listen to everything the Lord has commanded you to tell us' (v 33). It had an ideal preacher also. Peter began 'telling the good news of peace through Jesus Christ' (v.36). And it had, too, an ideal congregation who were eager and expectant, and as Peter spoke the Spirit came on them (v.44). If the Spirit is not at work in your church, don't necessarily blame the preacher; it may be because the congregation are not filled with expectation.

O God, I pray that when I gather with other believers may we always be expectant. In Jesus' name. Amen.

'Refined ineffectuality'

FOR READING AND MEDITATION
ACTS 19:1–7

'[Paul] asked them, "Did you receive the Holy Spirit when you believed?" They answered, "No ..."' (v.2)

In today's passage we see a Holy Spiritless type of religion – good on facts but lacking in power. Compare Apollos and Paul. The result of theological training without the Holy Spirit is to produce what someone has termed 'refined ineffectuality'. Many modern-day pulpits are occupied by people who have behind them years of training but no experience or dependence on the Spirit. The result? Refined ineffectuality and cultured emptiness. What a difference between the 'twelve' at Ephesus and the other 'Twelve' – the twelve apostles. The other Twelve were turning the world upside down; this 'twelve' were barely holding their own. Training and refinement may be good but they are no substitute for the Holy Spirit.

O God, give us men and women who will stand in the pulpit and preach in the power of the Spirit. In Jesus' name. Amen.

'This is My image'

FOR READING AND MEDITATION
ACTS 17:1–9

'These men who have caused trouble all over the world have now come here ...' (v.6)

C hrist in the flesh had great power, but Christ in His Church is even more powerful. Our Lord, working through the Holy Spirit, enabled His people to, 'turn the world upside down' (v.6, AV). God is concerned that in every age He should have people on earth who show the world what He is really like. He wants to say to every generation, 'This is My image.' He longs to indwell us and endue us in this century in the same way that He indwelt the Early Church. Dr Harry Ironside said, 'In the Early Church the Holy Spirit was the pulse beat of all they did – the Life of their living. In the Church of this century sometimes it is difficult to find a pulse at all.'

O God, help us not to settle for anything less than what we read about in the Acts of the Apostles. Revive us, dear Lord. In Jesus' name. Amen.

Feeding the mind

FOR READING AND MEDITATION
ACTS 2:42–47

'They devoted themselves to the apostles' teaching …' (v.42)

Another distinctive of the Early Church was: *their devotion to divine truth*. The first community of Christians was a learning and listening one. Clearly, the 3,000 new converts that came into the Church on the Day of Pentecost, plus the many others who were daily added to their number, found great delight in listening to the apostles as they unfolded the truths concerning Jesus Christ, the Lord. They did not become so taken up with the manifestations of the Spirit (as a number do today) that they despised the feeding of their minds. In my opinion in our church meetings we should not only find inspiration for our heart but also food for our mind.

Father, help me become as devoted to divine truth as were those first disciples. In Jesus' name. Amen.

The only reliable doctrine

FOR READING AND MEDITATION
1 JOHN 2:18–27

'... the anointing you received from him remains in you, and you do not need anyone to teach you.' (v.27)

S ome Christians refer to today's text and say something like this: 'Now I am filled with the Spirit, He is the only teacher I need. I can dispense with all human teachers. The Spirit alone is my Guide.' John was not ruling out human teachers, but combating the Gnostics, or 'Knowing Ones', who infiltrated the Early Church with false doctrine. He emphasised that what the Christians had been taught under the Spirit's ministry through the apostles was not only adequate, but was the only reliable doctrine. They needed nothing more than they had received through the Spirit's unfolding of the apostles' teaching. The teaching of the New Testament is the teaching of the apostles and today's true Christians will also be 'devoted ... to the apostles' teaching and to ... prayer' (Acts 2:42).

O God, thank You for inspiring the first apostles to lay down for us the truths by which we, Your Church, are to operate. Amen.

At the apostles' feet

FOR READING AND MEDITATION
ACTS 5:12–16

'And all the believers used to meet together in Solomon's Colonnade.' (v.12)

In order to get a feel of how important teaching was in the life of the Early Church permit me to take you on an imaginary trip into that first Christian community. Sometime after breakfast, everyone makes their way to Solomon's Colonnade on the east side of the Temple. When they arrive they sit on the floor with countless other new believers to worship God and listen to the teaching of the apostles. Imagine how they would have felt as they heard Peter or Matthew or John tell of the wealth they had inherited in Christ, and picture their faces as they listened to these men who had walked with Jesus unfolding so many wondrous truths concerning Him. How I wish I could have been there!

Father, give me an ever growing appetite for divine truth, I pray, for I know that without it I cannot develop as a Christian. Amen.

The best training ground

FOR READING AND MEDITATION
ACTS 7:1–16

'Brothers and fathers, listen to me!' (v.2)

Where did Stephen get all the knowledge and understanding as displayed in his sermon to the Sanhedrin? He got it, I imagine, first by studying the Scriptures for himself, but also by sitting at the apostles' feet, listening to the teaching that fell from their lips. Men and women of God are best prepared for future service by being involved in church life. Bible colleges are good, but they are no substitute for experiencing Christ in the community of the Church. The early disciples' main task was to experience daily the life of Christ as it was being worked out in His Church. These men and women were shaped by true Christian community – the best training ground I know.

Father, I am willing to be shaped by the community in which You have put me. Give me a teachable and responsive spirit I pray. Amen.

Slow but sure

FOR READING AND MEDITATION
ACTS 7:17–43

'... [Moses] received living words to pass on to us.' (v.38)

Stephen, Philip, Simeon and many others who were not apostles grew to great spiritual stature by experiencing Christ in His Church. They went through the stage of being new converts, rejoicing in their salvation, fellowshipping with other believers, and sitting at the feet of the apostles. Some Christians think that everything in the book of Acts happened in the space of about two years. Stephen probably preached his famous sermon to the Sanhedrin about three years after Pentecost, and the first missionary journey took place about 17 years after that great event! The Jerusalem believers were gradually equipped to live as God required them. They grew organically, steadily – the best way to grow.

Father, in an age when everything has to be 'instant', thank You for showing me the importance of slow and steady growth. Amen.

Another urgent need

FOR READING AND MEDITATION
ACTS 5:17–25

'Look! The men you put in jail are standing in the temple courts teaching the people.' (v.25)

When the apostles taught in the early years of the Church, they knew that Jesus had given them a unique authority, and the Church that existed in the period immediately after the apostles knew it also. What is tragic about some sections of today's Church is that they have lost all sense of biblical authority. Thus no clear message flows out from many modern pulpits. A true New Testament church is a biblical church – a church which believes the Bible, honours the Bible, teaches the Bible, and lives according to the Bible. Where the Bible is not opened the church speaks with a stutter. It may express opinions, but really, without the authority of the Bible, it simply has nothing to say.

O God, bring Your Church back once again to the Bible. Show us that without the Scriptures we have no real authority. In Jesus' name we pray. Amen.

Real community

FOR READING AND MEDITATION
1 JOHN 1:1–10

'But if we walk in the light, as he is in the light, we have fellowship with one another ...' (v.7)

Another distinctive of the Early Church was: *a deep sense of community and fellowship*. Immediately after Pentecost we read, 'They devoted themselves ... to the fellowship' (2:42, my emphasis). The Greek word for 'fellowship' is *koinonia* (pronounced coin own ia). This word can also be translated 'community' – and indicates living together as one family and having things in common. The coming of the Holy Spirit produced in the lives of the early Christians a spirit of oneness and unity that was quite remarkable. Today, generally speaking, the word 'fellowship' is used of a genial get-together of Christians, followed by coffee and biscuits. *Koinonia* goes far beyond that and is much deeper and much richer.

Father, I see that without koinonia *the Church is not at its best. Make us participants in true* koinonia. *For Jesus' sake we pray. Amen.*

'In constant review'

FOR READING AND MEDITATION
GALATIANS 2:1–10

'James, Peter and John … gave me and Barnabas the right hand of fellowship …' (v.9)

Anyone who reads Acts can see that there is a world of difference between the way the Early Church lived and the way we live today. A group of Christian students in a particular university carried out a survey of what their fellow students thought about Christ and the Church. The students were first asked to give an opinion on how they viewed Christ, and then on how they viewed the Church. Afterwards, when they analysed the survey, the Christian students got a shock. They found that only 5 per cent of those questioned were for the Church, yet 85 per cent said they were for Christ. I wonder why! Clearly we need to allow Christ to have free rein in His Church and experience *real* fellowship.

Father, help us see that one of the reasons why Christ died was so that His followers could enjoy true fellowship and communion. Amen.

Sharing in and sharing out

FOR READING AND MEDITATION
PHILIPPIANS 2:1–18

'If you have any encouragement from being united with Christ … if any fellowship with the Spirit …' (v.1)

*K*oinonia means fellowship, *koinonos* means partner, and *koinoneo* means to share. So those who partake in the *koinonia* are shareholders in a common concern. First, we share in the same inheritance – our eternal salvation. But *koinonia* is also something we share out. It has to do not only with what we possess, but what we do with what we possess. So what do we share with one another? We share everything God wants us to share. In the days immediately following Pentecost, Christians in Jerusalem were called to share their possessions with one another and to have everything in common. Although God may not call us to do the same thing today, this question remains: If He did, would we be willing?

Father, if self-interest has a strong hold on me then melt it by the power of Your love I pray. In Jesus' name. Amen.

Are you a 'good' Christian?

FOR READING AND MEDITATION
EPHESIANS 4:1–16

'... until we all reach unity in the faith and in the
knowledge of the Son of God ...' (v.13)

At least four aspects of Christian unity can be
observed in the Early Church. The first was *unity
with God*. If there is no unity with God then disharmony
spreads itself all down the line of human relationships.
The first Christians were so one with God that they
took on the significance of the One to whom they were
united. A second unity was *unity among themselves*.
Doubtless there were many strong personalities in the
Early Church but in the atmosphere of the Spirit, self-
centredness gives way to other-centredness. A good
Christian has been defined as 'one who gets along well
with others according to Jesus Christ'. How many of us,
I wonder (myself included), are 'good' Christians!

*Father, help me understand that unity is not something I
create; You have already created it through Christ and the
Holy Spirit. Amen.*

The results of unity

FOR READING AND MEDITATION
PSALM 133:1-3

'How good and pleasant it is when brothers live together in unity!' (v.1)

A third unity was *unity in their attitude to material possessions*. Today some Christians attempt to create the *koinonia* by getting together in a community and voluntarily sharing their possessions. But the sharing of possessions was not the cause of the *koinonia* – it was the result of it. A fourth unity was *the unity of all races*. At first the Early Church did show prejudice but eventually the Spirit prevailed. Look at this: 'In the church at Antioch there were prophets and teachers: Barnabas, Simeon called Niger …' (Acts 13:1). Simeon was a black man and possessed an important ministry gift in the church at Antioch. In Christ all racial prejudice has been laid to rest – forever.

O God, show us how we can restore this fourfold unity to the Church of the twenty-first century. In Jesus' name. Amen.

The Church as bread

FOR READING AND MEDITATION
I CORINTHIANS 10:14–33

'Because there is one loaf, we, who are many, are one body ...' (v.17)

In Acts 2:42 we read: 'They devoted themselves ...*to the breaking of bread...*' A loaf of bread speaks of the unity of the Church for at least four reasons. First, bread is a unity made up of many units. Second, it is the product of both earth and heaven. Earth produces the grain, but it needs rain from heaven to water it. Third, bread, like the Church, is not a luxury, but a necessity. We can manage without cake, but bread is a staple food. Fourth, bread can only fulfil its function through fraction. It is made to be broken. The Church, like bread, must be broken in God's hands if it is to be of service to the world. All this, and more, is in the simple but sacred act of the breaking of bread.

Father, thank You for all I receive at the communion table, but may the wonder of the unity of Your Body come home to me, too, Amen.

Is church life dangerous?

FOR READING AND MEDITATION
I CORINTHIANS 11:17–22

'... I have no praise for you, for your meetings do more harm than good.' (v.17)

To what extent is *koinonia* evident in the Church today? Not as fully as it should be. There are exceptions and there is a certain amount of love and friendliness in most Christian churches, but when measured against the *koinonia* of the New Testament – the commitment to share each other's lives in the deepest way possible – the Church of today seems a million miles off the mark. 'Going to some churches,' comments one writer, 'can be dangerous to your health.' While we thank God for those churches where true *koinonia* functions, there are far too many where backbiting, gossip, cliquishness and lack of consideration for others rules the day. True *koinonia* is the nearest thing to heaven on earth.

Father, mould Your present-day Church into a living fellowship which transcends all race and class and help us experience that true unity. For Christ's sake we ask it. Amen.

Praying and shaking

FOR READING AND MEDITATION
ACTS 4:23–31

'... they raised their voices together in prayer to God.' (v.24)

A further distinctive of the Early Church was: *the practice of persevering, believing prayer*. Their use of prayer was not limited to times of emergency only; often they prayed for a long while just for the joy of developing their relationship with their loving heavenly Father. Peter and John had been before the Sanhedrin and commanded not to speak any more in the name of Jesus (v.18). So when they are released what do they do? They go back to their fellow Christians, report the facts – and pray. Listen to their request: 'Enable your servants to speak your word with great boldness' (v.29). How did God answer their prayer? We read, 'The place where they were meeting was shaken', and they 'were all filled with the Holy Spirit and spoke the word of God boldly' (v.31).

O God, wake us up to the power that is available to us through fervent, believing prayer. In Jesus' name we ask it. Amen.

Paul learns to pray

FOR READING AND MEDITATION
ACTS 9:1–19

'... ask for a man from Tarsus named Saul, for he is praying.' (v.11)

Paul, who without doubt became one of the greatest prayer warriors of all time, learned to pray from the first moments of his conversion. Granted, his conversion was powerful and dramatic, but the point needs to be made nevertheless that the very first thing a new convert must do following his or her conversion is to learn to pray. Where and how we learn to pray is not important; what is important is that we do it, for without prayer there can be no onward march of progress in the Christian life. Saul of Tarsus had lost his physical vision, but he gained a new spiritual vision. To echo the words he uses in Ephesians 1:18, the eyes of his heart were gloriously opened.

My Father and my God, let this note go ringing through my soul today: my prayer moments are my greatest moments. Amen.

Locked in and locked out

FOR READING AND MEDITATION
ACTS 12:1–19

'[Rhoda] exclaimed, "Peter is at the door!" "You're out of your mind," they told her.' (vv.14–15)

When some of the Christians in Jerusalem heard that Peter had been imprisoned, they immediately went to the house of Mary, the mother of Mark, and began to pray. They prayed with great fervour and concern – so much so that God sent an angel into the prison to expedite Peter's escape. Once released, the apostle seemed to have more trouble getting into the prayer meeting than he did in getting out of prison! How strange that those who had gathered to pray found it hard to believe that God had actually answered their prayers. Strange, but yet quite normal for saints! I'm extremely glad God hears and answers those prayers that so often are mixed with unexpectancy and doubt.

Father, I am so grateful that You answer my prayers even when You foresee that I am going to react with incredulity and surprise when the answer comes. Amen.

The Church goes 'catholic'

FOR READING AND MEDITATION
ACTS 13:1–12

'So after they had fasted and prayed, they placed their hands on them and sent them off.' (v.3)

This is the section of Acts that tells us how the Church became catholic, and by 'catholic' I mean for everyone without distinction. The whole history of Western civilisation was redirected in that hour. Five men in the church at Antioch met together to fast and worship the Lord. As they did so, the Holy Spirit spoke to them. Once the Spirit had made known His will, they continued to fast and pray. If this same situation occurred in today's Church, upon hearing the Spirit's voice we would no doubt rise to take immediate action. These believers, however, sensed that Barnabas and Saul were about to enter an historic moment, and they needed to be sure everything they did was in tune with the will of God.

Father, teach me how to take every step in the atmosphere of believing prayer. Slow me down, dear Lord, that I might keep pace with Your purposes. Amen.

Power breaks through

FOR READING AND MEDITATION
ROMANS 12:9–21

'Be … faithful in prayer.' (v.12)

The modern-day Church has not stopped believing in the power of prayer, but it would be true to say that we are not as good as the Early Church at practising it. In my opinion the main reason why the Church of today does not experience the same degree of power in its midst as did the Early Church is because it does not give the same amount of time to prayer. At what point does the power of God break through into the life of the Church? God's power surges like a mighty ocean just waiting to find a point at which it can break through into the life of every Christian community. But the only point where it can break through is the point of prayer. When we pray a little then a little of God's power breaks through; when we pray a lot then a lot of His power breaks through. It is as simple as that.

O God, the reason why You want Your Church to pray is not to bring Your purposes in line with ours, but to bring our purposes in line with Yours. Amen.

The key doctrine

FOR READING AND MEDITATION
ACTS 2:22–41

'... God has made this Jesus, whom you crucified, both Lord and Christ.' (v.36)

The next distinctive is: *the emphasis which the believers placed on the Lordship of Christ*. Did you know that there are over 100 references in the book of Acts to the Lordship of Jesus Christ? The prominence given to this theme indicates that this is an issue of tremendous spiritual importance. John Stott, in a sermon he gave one year at the Keswick Convention, said, 'If I were to ask you what is the master key doctrine in the Scriptures, I wonder what you would answer? The sovereignty of God? The cross? The fullness of the Spirit? I would argue that the master key is ... the Lordship of Christ.' I agree. You see, no one can be a disciple of Christ, unless he or she submits to Christ's Lordship.

O God, thank You that Your Son is both our Saviour and our Lord. Amen.

A shock to the system

FOR READING AND MEDITATION
ACTS 22:1–16

*'"Who are you, Lord?" I asked. "I am Jesus of Nazareth,
whom you are persecuting," he replied.' (v.8)*

F ocusing still on the theme of Christ's Lordship, we
look once again at the conversion of Saul of Tarsus.
The thing, so I believe, that had such a profound effect
upon Saul was not the blinding light but the illumination
that came to his soul concerning Jesus of Nazareth.
Previously he thought that Jesus was just a carpenter
from Nazareth; now he saw that He was none other
than the Lord of the universe. It was a shock to both his
spiritual and physical systems. But he came through it
to be the greatest exponent of Christ's Lordship that the
world has ever seen.

*Father, I am so thankful that You brought Saul into Your
kingdom, and for the fact that his conversion still converts.
Amen.*

Jesus – Saviour and Lord

FOR READING AND MEDITATION
ACTS 16:16–40

'Believe in the Lord Jesus, and you will be saved – you and your household.' (v.31)

When the jailer sees that the prisoners have not fled, he asks Paul, 'What must I do to be saved?' (v.30). Paul replies, 'Believe in the Lord Jesus, and you will be saved.' Consider Paul's words: 'Believe in the Lord Jesus ...' In the days of Paul and the other apostles, converts were introduced immediately to the truth of Christ's Lordship. There was no suggestion that they could accept Christ as Saviour and then, at some point in the future, commit themselves to Him as Lord. The Early Church spoke with one voice when it gave converts this message: if you want to be saved then you must acknowledge Christ's Lordship over the whole of your life. There is no other form of salvation.

O God, help Your Church share its message that Jesus is both Lord and Saviour. In Jesus' name. Amen.

Biblical evangelism

FOR READING AND MEDITATION
ACTS 28:17–31

*'... he preached the kingdom of God and taught about
the Lord Jesus Christ.' (v.31)*

It's always been a matter of great interest to me that
the last four words of the final verse of Acts are these:
'the Lord Jesus Christ'. We are quite wrong when, in
our modern-day evangelism, we present the gospel in
a way that suggests the important thing is only finding
forgiveness for one's sin. The real issue, the greater issue,
is committing oneself to the living Lord. Forgiveness of
sins is necessary before one can live in harmony with
Christ, but important though the forgiveness of sins is
– and let no one minimise it – what is of even greater
importance is the commitment to Christ as Lord.
Evangelism that does not make this clear is not worthy
of the name. It is evanjellyism.

*O God, deliver us from any confusion on this matter. Show
us that You cannot be our Saviour unless we are willing to
acknowledge You as our Lord. Amen.*

Mutiny in the ranks?

FOR READING AND MEDITATION
LUKE 6:43–49

'Why do you call me, "Lord, Lord," and do not do what I say?' (v.46)

This is the acid test of Christianity: obedience to Christ as Lord. Look around the Church at the moment and ask yourself: Who is calling the shots? Is it the Commander or the troops? The soldiers or the General? In today's Church, one of our greatest problems is mutiny in the ranks. If we say we believe Christ is Lord but do not rely on His strength to enable us to do what He calls us to do then we are merely paying Him lip service. Let me remind you of a statement I have used many times before: if we do not crown Him Lord of all, we do not crown Him Lord at all.

Father, I don't want to be an insubordinate member of Your Church. Help me put my words into action. Amen.

The greatest of all rooms

FOR READING AND MEDITATION
ACTS 2:1

'When the day of Pentecost came, they were all together in one place.' (v.1)

An article in an American magazine had as its title, 'Little rooms where new worlds were made'. It talked about some of the great rooms of history and the new worlds that have been created from them. There was the chamber in Philadelphia where the *Declaration of Independence* was signed; the room in London where Karl Marx wrote his communist classic, *Das Kapital*; the room in St Leonards on Sea where John Logie Baird succeeded in producing television. The article spoke of many other rooms, but by far the greatest of all rooms was that in which 120 disciples of Christ met in the days leading up to the Day of Pentecost (see Acts 1:15). From that room came the beginnings of a new society – the Church.

O God, as at Pentecost, breathe Your fire once again into my life. I ask that You will touch me afresh. Holy Spirit, come and fill me to overflowing. Amen.

A sense of the numinous

FOR READING AND MEDITATION
ACTS 4:32–36

'With great power the apostles continued to testify to the resurrection of the Lord Jesus ...' (v.33)

Another distinctive of the Early Church that made it such a spiritual force and power was this: *it had a strong and pervading sense of the numinous.* The word 'numinous' doesn't appear very much in evangelical writings, but it was a favourite word of men such as C.S. Lewis, George MacDonald and Rudolph Otto. The dictionary defines it as 'sensing the presence of divinity; awe-inspiring'. It is a word that conveys the holy fear we ought to experience when we become aware of our creaturehood, and realise that we stand in the presence of a holy God. There can be no real knowledge of God unless there is the sense of the numinous. The Early Church experienced it. So must we.

Gracious and loving Father, may I sense Your awe-inspiring presence more and more. In Jesus' name. Amen.

Two out of fellowship

FOR READING AND MEDITATION
ACTS 5:1–11

'Great fear seized the whole church and all who heard about these events.' (v.11)

Ananias and Sapphira were perfectly free to do what they liked with their money – to give it to the Church or keep it for themselves – but they were not free to lie. Their root sin was hypocrisy, and it swiftly brought upon them the judgment of God. But why was the penalty so severe? Because God wanted to show His people that the *koinonia* was not to be taken lightly. However slow to come to judgment God would appear in later times, this first sin against the Body could not go unpunished. If you ever need to be reminded of what God really thinks about hypocrisy then turn to Acts 5. What happened to Ananias and Sapphira stands for all time as a warning of how seriously God views the defilement of His Body.

My Father, help me see that Your abhorrence of sin, like Your nature, is the same 'yesterday, today and forever'. Amen.

Overcoming power

FOR READING AND MEDITATION
ACTS 19:8–20

*'... they were all seized with fear, and the name of the
Lord Jesus was held in high honour.' (v.17)*

Ephesus was the seat of magic, exorcism and belief in
the powers of darkness. Paul worked extraordinary
miracles there in order to demonstrate that the Jesus he
proclaimed was greater than the prince of the powers of
darkness. As a result of what happened to the sons of
Sceva, who used Christ's name without His authority,
the whole community was seized with fear, and a great
spiritual move took place. Many Ephesians confessed
their performance of magical practices. The evidence that
God's power was at work in the Early Church, overcoming
every power set against Him, clearly contributed to a
sense of the numinous. How desperately we need that
same power to be at work in our churches today.

*O God, we have come too far to turn back now. Remain
with us, dear Lord, so that we see Pentecostal days again.
Amen.*

A developing trend

FOR READING AND MEDITATION
ACTS 17:16–34

'… he himself gives all men life and breath and everything else.' (v.25)

The first Christians were in awe of God and rightly feared Him. When we lose a sense of reverence for God we soon find ourselves rationalising His commands, adapting His words to suit ourselves, and cauterising our consciences. There is a fine line between being God's friend and being too much in awe of Him, but we need to be careful that familiarity does not breed contempt. I am concerned about the way in which God is viewed by some Christians today – how He is trivialised, packaged for entertainment, seen as a formula for success, or treated like a celestial slot machine. Personally, I do not know how it is possible to talk meaningfully about a God before whose glory we have not first trembled.

O God, help me always to be in awe of You. Your own Son knew You better than anyone, yet called You 'holy Father'. Amen.

The way to worship

FOR READING AND MEDITATION
HEBREWS 12:14–29

'… worship God acceptably with reverence and awe, for our "God is a consuming fire."' (vv.28–29)

We must be careful not to make references to God that demean Him. I am not arguing that we should lose the sense of familiarity that flows from the relationship we have as a son or daughter with our loving Father (God forbid!). But why should we be afraid of Someone we love? Doesn't the Bible tell us, 'There is no fear in love,' and that 'perfect love drives out fear' (1 John 4:18)? Yes, it does, but it is talking about a kind of fear that is different to the one I have been describing over these past few days. The fear I am talking about is a godly fear – a healthy reverence and respect for the position and power of the Almighty.

O God, help us draw close to You in love yet maintain a respect and an awe for You that recognises how great You really are. Amen.

Dangerous criticism

FOR READING AND MEDITATION
ACTS 6:1–7

'... the Grecian Jews ... complained against the Hebraic
Jews because their widows were being overlooked ...' (v.1)

Another distinctive of the Early Church was: *the
ability to reconcile or hold together in unbroken
fellowship strong people who differed.* The Living Bible
says: 'there were rumblings of discontent'. The Greek
word for 'rumblings' is *gongusmos*, meaning 'a complaint
expressed in subdued tones'. In other words, secret
criticism. There is nothing wrong with criticism that is
open and honest. Criticism is dangerous, however, when
it is expressed covertly and not brought out into the
open Fellowship is based on confidence; secret criticism
breaks that confidence. The apostles acted promptly, and
thus saved the situation. Nothing must be allowed to
mar the unity of the Body. Nothing.

*Father, please give the leaders of Your Church the courage
and confidence to deal with every issue that threatens the
unity of Your Body. Amen.*

No place for prejudice

FOR READING AND MEDITATION
ACTS 11:1–18

'... they ... praised God, saying, "So then, God has granted even the Gentiles repentance unto life."' (v.18)

As they listened to Peter, they could not help but be moved, and concluded with him that 'God has granted even the Gentiles repentance unto life'. It wasn't easy for Peter to go to the home of Cornelius, a Gentile, and it wasn't easy for the Jewish Christians to admit Gentiles. The fact that they did is a tremendous testimony to their openness and responsiveness to the work of the Holy Spirit, who was moving in their midst. Bigotry and prejudice at this critical moment in the life of the Early Church could have brought it to a halt. How wonderful it would be if bigotry and prejudice were dealt with as easily in the modern-day Church as they were in this.

Father, give us such an experience of the Holy Spirit, that we will have the ability to hold together strong people who differ. Amen.

'You need grace!'

FOR READING AND MEDITATION
ACTS 15:36–41

'They had such a sharp disagreement that they parted company.' (v.39)

J.B. Phillips translates today's verse: 'There was a sharp clash of opinion, so much so that they went their separate ways.' This split could easily have led to the start of two denominations – the Paulites, who believed the Church should be for fully committed and reliable believers, and the Barnabites, who believed people should be given another chance. Holders of both views might well have felt justified in starting a different denomination, but thankfully this did not happen. When Paul and Silas – the man Paul chose to replace Barnabas – departed on their journey, they were 'commended by the brothers to the grace of the Lord'. For it's only grace that can keep strong men pulling together.

Father, let Your grace flow in and prevail in Your Church when strong spiritual men and women differ. In Jesus' name. Amen.

'A grand Christian'

FOR READING AND MEDITATION
2 TIMOTHY 4:1–18

'Get Mark and bring him with you, because he is helpful to me in my ministry.' (v.11)

One writer suggests that when Paul sat down in later years and dictated the words of our text today, the scribe might have looked up with a quizzical smile as if to say, 'You really mean that? Mark helpful in your ministry?' Whereupon Paul possibly replied, 'Yes, he is – and Barnabas had much to do with that. Barnabas was a better Christian than me. He was always taking up with people no one else would associate with. He pleaded my cause when nobody believed in me. A grand Christian, Barnabas.' Perhaps a tear then trickled down his cheek. Whatever had gone wrong in the past, it was now forgiven and forgotten. Happily, the sharp dissension between Barnabas and Paul had been healed.

Father, how good it is when sharp divisions between Christians are forgiven and forgotten. Please help me restore any broken relationships. Amen.

Disagreeing agreeably

FOR READING AND MEDITATION
2 CORINTHIANS 5:11–21

'… God … has committed to us the message of
reconciliation.' (v.19)

Today's Church does not appear to be as effective at
reconciling differences as were the early Christians.
Huge divisions split our churches. And the difficulty is
not so much that Christians disagree – but that they
disagree disagreeably. It ought to be possible for those
who are 'in Christ' to maintain a loving spirit even
though they see things from different points of view.
Strong people will differ, and sometimes differ sharply,
but the Church must always point them to the way of
reconciliation. Any church that does not do that is not
following the example set by the Church of the New
Testament. Reconciliation is the heart of the gospel; all
else is subsidiary.

*O God, please bring Your Church to the place where it is
a redeeming and a reconciling community. Help us, dear
Father. In Jesus' name. Amen.*

The first Christian martyr

FOR READING AND MEDITATION
ACTS 7:51–60

'While they were stoning him, Stephen prayed, "Lord Jesus, receive my spirit."' (v.59)

Another characteristic of the Early Church was this: *there was no distinction between what today we call the laity and the clergy.* Although the book Luke wrote is called 'The Acts of the Apostles', it records some significant things which were done by people who were not apostles. Stephen was such a man from the ranks – a layman. We are told he was 'full of faith and of the Holy Spirit' (6:5), and 'full of God's grace and power' (6:8). Standing in the crowd, 'holding the coats', was Saul of Tarsus. I don't think he ever forgot the sight of Stephen's radiant face as the stones pounded the life out of him. I have no doubt that occasion was one of many events that led to his conversion.

Father, drive deep within me the truth that the Christian spirit always wins. And for that I am eternally grateful. Amen.

'Philip the Evangelist'

FOR READING AND MEDITATION
ACTS 8:4–13,26–40

'Philip went down to a city in Samaria and proclaimed the Christ there.' (v.5)

A nother great Christian layman was Philip. He was one the group chosen to 'wait on tables' (6:3–4). But the reach of Philip's soul went beyond the reach of his hand; he wanted to have a share in the distribution of the gospel as well as the distribution of goods. Philip was a man whose evangelistic impulse was exerted in and through and beyond his occupation. He is an inspiration to all those businessmen and women who yearn to serve the Lord. To have a firm hold on the basic truths of the gospel, and to feel responsibility for sharing it with others, is to stand in the splendid tradition of this great layman who, over the years, has earned the distinction of being known as 'Philip the Evangelist'.

O God, this is indeed the greatest work in the world. No matter what my role in life, help me to see my most important task is sharing Jesus. Amen.

'Son of Encouragement'

FOR READING AND MEDITATION
ACTS 9:19–31

'When he came to Jerusalem, he tried to join the disciples, but they were all afraid of him ...' (v.26)

B arnabas, whose name means 'Son of Encouragement' (4:36), another layman, had a large heart and a magnanimous spirit, especially where people needed help. The first appearance of Barnabas is in Acts 4:36–37, where we see him selling his land and bringing the money to lay at the apostles' feet. He appears next in 9:26–27, where we observe him befriending Saul of Tarsus and introducing him to the apostles in Jerusalem. Then, in 11:25–26, we see him seeking out Paul to be his co-worker. Barnabas was large-hearted in his treatment of a man who needed acceptance and couldn't get it. It's sad when Christian disciples are so orthodox in their theology but so enamelled in their sympathy.

Father, help me never to be hard and unforgiving to people who were involved in some terrible sin before they came to know You. In Jesus' name. Amen.

A place for everyone

FOR READING AND MEDITATION
I CORINTHIANS 12:12–31

'Now you are the body of Christ, and each one of you is a part of it.' (v.27)

The Church here in the twenty-first century needs to take note that when Jesus said to the disciples, 'As the Father has sent me, I am sending you [or apostling you]' (John 20:21), He was commissioning the whole Church. Christ, the Head of the Church, has a use for every one of us in His Body. There are still people in some sections of the Church who think that the ministers who operate from the front of the church are the only ones who should do the work of Christ. Once, while ministering in Malaysia, I preached in a church where the printed notice sheet had on it these words: 'Ministers – the entire congregation.' I glowed inwardly as I thought, 'You've got it.'

Show me, dear Lord, just what You want me to do, and where You want me to be. In Christ's name I pray. Amen.

Church growth

FOR READING AND MEDITATION
ACTS 4:1–12

'But many who heard the message believed, and the number of men grew to about five thousand.' (v.4)

*T*he first Church was a growing Church to which converts were added in ever increasing numbers. There were 120 in the upper room and at Pentecost another 3,000 believed. From then on, souls were added to the Church daily (2:47). Later we read that the number of men grew to 5,000. Please notice that the figure given here is only for the men, and we can assume that about the same number of women also became committed followers of the Christ. In Acts 5:14 and 6:7 still more growth is recorded. Some Church historians reckon that just four weeks after Pentecost there must have been around 12,000 to 15,000 converts in the Early Church. Now that's Church growth! And there was more to follow.

O Father, as I reflect on the wave after wave of converts who streamed into the Early Church, my heart cries out: Do it again, dear Lord, do it again. Amen.

God has no energy crisis

FOR READING AND MEDITATION
ACTS 4:23 –30

*'Stretch out your hand to heal and perform miraculous
signs and wonders …' (v.30)*

The post-Pentecost period is filled with accounts
of wonderful events, such as outstanding healings
(even from standing in Peter's shadow, 5:15), a building
being shaken by the power of God (4:31), prison doors
opening of their own accord (5:19; 12:10), two people
being struck down dead because of their deception
(5:1–10), and so on. There can be little doubt that the
supernaturalism in the Early Church had a tremendous
pulling power on the hearts of the people. But can we
expect similar manifestations today? Ah, here the Church
is divided. Personally, I believe we can. God doesn't have
an energy crisis. His Spirit still works in great power in
some parts of the world today. Why not where we are?

*Yes Father – why not? Can it be that we are more problem
conscious than power conscious? Shake us up, dear Lord.
In Jesus' name. Amen.*

No place for the spurious

FOR READING AND MEDITATION
JOHN 14:1–15

' ... anyone who has faith in me will do what I have been doing. He will do even greater things than these ...' (v.12)

I believe God intends the supernatural and the miraculous to be as much part of today's Church as it was of the Early Church. However I must add that I deplore the fact that where there is no evidence of the supernatural and the truly miraculous, people try to create it by psychological means. In Bible days it wasn't the apostles or evangelists who made a fuss about healing, but the people who were healed! Think, for instance, of the lame man at the Beautiful Gate (Acts 3:8–10). Personally, I ache to see the supernatural power of God at work in His Church today – just as it was in Bible days. But I abhor what is the spurious. And perhaps it's the spurious that is stopping the reality coming through.

O God, if it is the spurious that is holding back the pure stream of Your Spirit then flush it out. Give us once again the pure stream of Pentecost. Amen.

The peril of second best

FOR READING AND MEDITATION
ACTS 6:1–7

'So the word of God spread … and a large number of priests became obedient to the faith.' (v.7)

The apostles were led by the Spirit to differentiate between the good and the best. What they were doing in administration was good, but it was not the best. The best was to give themselves to God in prayer and concentrate on presenting the Word in a clear and effective way. One of the devil's favourite devices is to get Christ's servants engaged in doing things that are second best, thus robbing them of their real cutting edge. How many modern churches, I wonder, have fallen into the trap of expecting their spiritual leaders to be estate agents, transport managers, financial advisers, and so on, rather than ministers of the Word? Today's Church must be keenly aware of the peril of the second best.

O God, how desperately we need the wisdom of the Spirit, for sometimes it is terribly difficult to differentiate between the good and the best. Amen.

A domestic context

FOR READING AND MEDITATION
ACTS 5:29–42

*'Day after day … they never stopped teaching and
proclaiming the good news …' (v.42)*

Another factor that contributed to the phenomenal
growth of the Early Church was the way in
which the disciples met in small groups (2:46). They
supplemented the large services with more informal
meetings in their homes. Every healthy local church
should not only have large united services on Sundays
but should also divide the congregation into fellowship
groups which meet in homes during the week. Those
who do this, and who invite along those who are not yet
Christians, say unbelievers appear to be more ready to
receive Christ in a home than they do in a formal church.
What a ministry can come out of a home where Christ
is the Head and where the doors are open to those who
do not yet know Him.

*My Father and my God, You see Your Church not as a brick
building but as a living Body. Help me to see it in the same
way. Amen.*

Original-style evangelism

FOR READING AND MEDITATION
ACTS 8:1–8

'When the crowds heard Philip and saw the miraculous signs he did, they all paid close attention to what he said.' (v.6)

The Early Church expanded in the way it did for three primary reasons: the presence of the supernatural, the powerful teaching of the apostles, and the daily witness of the believers in their homes. And this went on in spite of the problems the Church faced, which included strong opposition and internal complaints. One of the main ministries of the Church was establishing those who became believers and modelling for all time what can happen when the people of God dwell together in unity. History and experience have shown us that the most powerful and successful evangelistic efforts are those made by a church that knows true *koinonia* and real spiritual unity. That kind of evangelism never fails.

Father, help us understand that we cannot be evangelical without being evangelistic and a church in unity is evangelism according to Your pattern. Amen.

Another King

FOR READING AND MEDITATION
ACTS 5:25–32

'Peter and the other apostles replied: "We must obey God rather than men!"' (v.29)

The last on our list of the Early Church's distinctive is: *their unswerving allegiance to Christ and His eternal kingdom*. The first Christians, whilst maintaining respect for the civil authorities that were over them, saw that their primary allegiance was to the laws and principles of the kingdom of God. They were not anarchists, but sought to run their lives in harmony with the truths being taught by the apostles. We are expected to live in obedience to earthly authorities until we are asked to do something contrary to God's commands. The apostles were not out to overthrow the systems of their day; they were simply men who knew that their first allegiance was to Jesus Christ and His kingdom.

Our Father and our God, we come to You once again to ask that You will help us get our priorities right. Amen.

A right response

FOR READING AND MEDITATION
ACTS 23:1–11

'Paul replied, "Brothers, I did not realise that he was the high priest …"' (v.5)

S ome commentators claim that the Early Church, being 'God's new society', had a complete disregard for the old systems of authority and government. However, the passage before us now shows that viewpoint to be false. Paul felt hurt and angry by the command of the high priest, but when he discovered that he was talking to a man with spiritual authority, he knew that he was called upon by God to proffer respect. But how could Paul respect a man who had just ordered him to be hit across the mouth? There was only one way this was possible. He did it by focusing not so much on the person but on his position and therefore the principle of authority.

O God, I see that a right response to authority is one of our supreme responsibilities. Please help us to respect all authority. Amen.

A different drum

FOR READING AND MEDITATION
ROMANS 12:1–8

'Do not conform any longer to the pattern of this world ...'
(v.2)

The Church of the first century marched through the world to the beat of a different drum. Maybe you are familiar with the words of the American essayist, Thoreau, who said, 'If a man does not keep pace with his companions perhaps it's because he hears a different drummer. Let him step to the music he hears however measured or far away.' The beat the early Christians listened to came not from around, but from above. Their spiritual ears were tuned in to the music of heaven, and they tried to keep in step with that, even though it brought them into direct conflict with the world. How different things would be if this were the case today.

O Father, help Your Church today to march to the beat of heaven's music, and not to be influenced by the ideas of the world. Amen.

True nonconformity

FOR READING AND MEDITATION
ACTS 8:18–24

'Peter answered: "May your money perish with you, because you thought you could buy the gift of God with money!"' (v.20)

Simon Peter and others in the Early Church stood out against the trends and ideas of their day. While Malcolm Muggeridge was Rector of Edinburgh University he discovered that the university authorities were planning to give out free contraceptives to students. Since no effort was being made to convince students of the deleterious effects of pre-marital sex, he decided that as a Christian he should resign. His farewell address was widely reported. Malcolm Muggeridge ended his speech from the pulpit of St Giles' Cathedral in Edinburgh with these powerful words: 'The reason why I resign from my duties today is because I cannot go along with this. I belong to another kingdom and to another King – one Jesus.'

O God may I have the courage to stand up for You if I find the laws of the world conflict with Your laws. In Jesus' name I pray. Amen.

Picking up the beat

FOR READING AND MEDITATION
1 PETER 1:3–25

'As obedient children, do not conform to the evil desires you had when you lived in ignorance.' (v.14)

Without belittling the many positive things the Church is doing, it remains true that when compared to the Church of the first century it is disunited, enfeebled and in retreat. The gates of hell seem to prevail even though we know that Christ promises they will not. We must stop trying to be trendy and become more transformative. The Church is not being condemned by the world because it is like Christ; it is being condemned because it is not like Him. When we stop trying to keep in step with the music of the world, and march to the beat of a different drum, we will make a far more powerful impression. Again I say: the greatest challenge of our time is to pick up heaven's beat – and follow it.

O Father, once again we pray, help us not to conform to the standards of the world, but to march to the beat of heaven's drum. Amen.

The return

FOR READING AND MEDITATION
JEREMIAH 6:9–20

'This is what the LORD says: "Stand at the crossroads and look; ask for the ancient paths …"' (v.16)

We must think not only about how we can develop new programmes for the future but also how we can return to the old paths – to the sincerity, eagerness and enthusiasm of those first-century Christians. When we see how the Church was meant to function, we can more easily spot the deviations. There are cultural differences between us and them of course, but we must not use the cultural differences as an excuse for failing to see the spiritual differences. Every local church ought to go often to the book of Acts and take whatever steps are necessary to make their fellowship a living illustration of what community life in Christ is like. Let's dedicate ourselves afresh to God and *His* kingdom.

Father, having seen how Your Church should function, my prayer and deepest longing is this: give us another Pentecost. In Jesus' name we pray. Amen.

Meet your Designer

FOR READING AND MEDITATION
COLOSSIANS 1:15–23

'For by him all things were created: things in heaven and on earth … all things were created by him and for him.' (v.16)

For the next few weeks we shall consider what a Christian needs to know and do in order to have a soul that is filled with the deepest possible happiness and is truly blessed of God. No one knows the soul better than Jesus because He designed it. But what exactly is the soul? A basic definition is this: the soul is the part of us with which we think, feel and decide, or, to put it another way, our thoughts, feelings and will. There are three views we can have of the soul: (1) that the soul is naturally Christian; (2) that the soul is naturally pagan; (3) that the soul is naturally half pagan and half Christian. I vote for the first view. We are image bearers – in whom the image of God has been marred by sin.

Lord Jesus Christ, when I met You I knew that I had met the One for whom I was fashioned. In You I find my self – my real self. Amen.

A prescription for health

FOR READING AND MEDITATION
MATTHEW 5:1–12

*'Now when he saw the crowds, he went up on a
mountainside and sat down.' (v.1)*

Jesus identifies the attitudes necessary for the soul
to function as it should, and they are the best
prescription for spiritual and mental health it is possible
to find. These eight crisp and powerful statements give
us the irreducible minimum we need for our souls to
work in Christ's way. What Jesus presents here are
positive attitudes, and that is why we call them 'the
Be-attitudes', or 'Declarations of Blessedness', or, if you
prefer, 'the Beautiful Attitudes'. Each statement begins
with the word 'blessed', so it follows that if you want
your life to be blessed then the more fully you adopt
these attitudes, the happier you will be.

*Lord Jesus Christ, I see that You have created me to live in
harmony with Your will and to adopt Your attitudes. Lead
on, dear Master. Amen.*

Body and soul – integrated

FOR READING AND MEDITATION
ROMANS 13:8–14

'... clothe yourselves with the Lord Jesus Christ, and do not think about how to gratify the desires of the sinful nature.' (v.14)

Our age is fascinated with psychology and mental wellbeing. There is, however, only one true psychology – what I describe as the psychology of Jesus. Please don't be put off by the term 'psychology' because it simply means 'a study and understanding of the working of the soul'. And who better to understand the soul than Jesus? It is my firm belief that the teaching contained in the Beatitudes is the finest prescription for mental, emotional and spiritual health ever given. God has so designed us that the right attitudes produce the right effects in our bodies. It is helpful to keep in mind that they are 'be attitudes' and not 'do attitudes'. The doing comes out of the being.

Gracious Father, I see You have made us in such a way that the right things are good for us and bad things are bad for us. Amen.

Restructured thinking

FOR READING AND MEDITATION
ROMANS 12:1–8

'Do not conform any longer to the pattern of this world, but be transformed by the renewing of your mind.' (v.2)

One of the most popular approaches by psychologists to helping troubled souls nowadays is what is called 'cognitive restructuring'. Wrong thoughts are challenged and then changed to ones which are more helpful. Dr James Fisher, a psychiatrist who carried out research into the positive qualities that make for good mental health, said, 'I dreamed of writing a handbook that would be simple, practical, and easy to follow; it would tell people how to live – what thoughts and attitudes and philosophies to cultivate and what pitfalls to avoid in seeking good mental health. And quite by accident I discovered that such a work had been completed – the Beatitudes.' What an admission!

Father, I long not just to live, but to live abundantly. This is what You promise me through Your Son. Help me to learn, listen and obey. Amen.

The gateway to happiness

FOR READING AND MEDITATION
PSALM 68:1–10

'... may the righteous be glad and rejoice before God;
may they be happy and joyful.' (v.3)

O ur attitudes determine our altitude – how high we
rise in spiritual maturity and emotional fulfilment.
There can be no doubt that the Beatitudes are the gateway
to spiritual health and happiness. Decide here and now
that you will not rest until the 'Be attitudes' become part
of your daily thinking and daily living. If every Christian
could adopt the eight attitudes which Jesus identifies for
us in the Beatitudes then, other things being equal, I am
convinced there would not be an unhappy or unfulfilled
person in the Christian Church. One wonders why it
is that the Church, which possesses such a powerful
blueprint for healthy and abundant living, does not make
more of it.

*Father, I am so grateful that You have led me to this gateway
to health and happiness. Help me walk through it carefully,
prayerfully and expectantly. Amen.*

A serious misconception

FOR READING AND MEDITATION
MALACHI 3:6–18

'But now we call the arrogant blessed.' (v.15)

The Jews of Malachi's day were so warped and twisted in their thinking that they equated arrogance with being blessed. They thought that those who put themselves first were the happy or blessed ones. That's how the Old Testament finishes – with a misconception of what it means to be blessed of God. After this, for 400 years, the nation of Israel went through a dark period during which no prophet's voice was heard in the land. Then Jesus came. And in one of His first sermons – the Sermon on the Mount – He spelt out in detail and in crystal clear terms exactly what it means to be blessed of God. Arrogance is not the way to a blessed life – humility is.

Gracious and loving heavenly Father, thank You for opening up to us a new approach to life. In Christ's name. Amen.

Under His blessing

FOR READING AND MEDITATION
EPHESIANS 1:1–14

'Praise be to the God and Father of our Lord Jesus Christ, who has blessed us ... with every spiritual blessing in Christ.' (v.3)

As we focus on each of the Beatitudes I shall use a supplementary reading to broaden our biblical understanding. In this first statement Jesus puts His finger on one of the most vital issues in life – personal satisfaction and joy; in other words, living out our lives under the blessing of God. However, although it is God's desire that His children should experience happiness and enjoy His blessing in their lives, it is important for us to understand that it is only when we live in harmony with God and follow His principles that our souls can experience the blessing He has for us. There can be no real and true satisfaction in the soul which depends for its pleasure and joy on things other than God.

Thank You, my Father, that You desire my happiness. I desire it too. Help me stay close to You all my days. In Jesus' name. Amen.

'Straining at the oars'

FOR READING AND MEDITATION
MARK 6:45–51

'He saw the disciples straining at the oars, because the wind was against them.' (v.48)

True contentment is not something you manufacture, but something you receive. Contentment is a coquette; follow her and she eludes you; turn from her and interest yourself in something or someone else and you may win her. Scripture and our modern-day psychologists are one here. The disciples were 'straining at the oars', rowing in the dark and getting nowhere. The account in John's Gospel tells us that when the disciples took Jesus into the boat, 'immediately the boat reached the shore where they were heading' (John 6:21). This is how it is with contentment. When we strive to achieve it we 'strain at the oars'. But when we let Christ in, lo, we are at the place where we were heading.

Father, I see that to get contentment I must 'forget' it. It is not an achievement but a by-product of knowing You. Amen.

Help!

FOR READING AND MEDITATION
JOHN 13:1–17

'Now that you know these things, you will be blessed if you do them.' (v.17)

I n this first Beatitude our Lord is not thinking of material poverty, but spiritual poverty. Look again at Jesus' words: 'Blessed are the poor *in spirit* ...' (Matt.5:3). The word for 'poor' in the Greek is *ptochos* – a word that is also used of those reduced to begging, those who are dependent on others. Here it implies a voluntary emptying of our inner being in order to receive something of greater benefit. We are willing to empty our hands of our own possessions and abilities and have them filled with the riches of God. Contentment begins then with self-renunciation. We must humbly acknowledge that we cannot find the blessed life through our own efforts. We need help – God's help.

Father, enable me to understand that in Your kingdom it is only the empty who receive. And so I empty myself to be filled by You. Amen.

Receptivity

FOR READING AND MEDITATION
JOHN 1:1–14

*'Yet to all who received him ... he gave the right to
become children of God ...' (v.12)*

The first law of life is receptivity, and that is also the
first law of the kingdom of heaven. How do we get the
right to become children of God? First, by receptivity – *'to
all who received him'*. At the very threshold of Christ's
kingdom we are met with the demand for self-emptying.
We should not consider it strange that entrance into the
kingdom of God begins with receptivity. Isn't that where
all life begins? The seed sown in the ground needs to
receive moisture and nutriments from the earth before it
can grow and produce flowers or fruit. Life that doesn't
begin with receptivity just doesn't begin.

*O God, help me respond to You. I open my life afresh to You
today. In Christ's name. Amen.*

Life: a response to environment

FOR READING AND MEDITATION
PSALM 149:1–9

'For the LORD takes delight in his people; he crowns the humble with salvation.' (v.4)

L ife has been defined as 'a response to environment'. We live physically when we respond to our physical environment by breathing in oxygen, drinking fluids and eating food. When that response is shut off then we die physically. Take a plant; how does it live? By being proud, self-sufficient, unrelated and unresponsive? No, it lives by surrendering, adjusting, receiving. Jesus is saying in the first of the Beatitudes that we must humbly choose to give up the idea that we can make life work on our own, and allow Him to flood our lives with His presence and power. To find contentment and happiness we must find Christ. But we will never find Him unless first we are willing to relinquish our pride.

O God my Father, give me a spirit that is humble and responsive to You I pray. In Jesus' name. Amen.

Thronging vs touching

FOR READING AND MEDITATION
LUKE 8:40–56

'She came up behind him and touched the edge of his cloak, and immediately her bleeding stopped.' (v.44)

There is a great difference between thronging Jesus and touching Him. Every week thousands go in and out of our churches, join in the activities, sing the hymns and choruses, listen to the sermon; they throng Jesus but never touch Him. I wonder, am I speaking now to someone just like this? Do you go to church regularly, mingle with the worshippers and, to a certain degree, enjoy the atmosphere of spirituality and worship – but never touch Jesus? If this is so, reach out and touch Him now. Touch Him for forgiveness, for inner cleansing, for power over temptation, for victory over fears and everything that stands in the way of being blessed by God. Cease thronging Him and reach out and touch Him – today.

Lord Jesus Christ, I reach out now to touch You with the hand of faith. My needs are great, but I know You are greater than them all. Amen.

Candidates for the kingdom

FOR READING AND MEDITATION
EPHESIANS 2:1–10

*'For it is by grace you have been saved, through faith –
and this not from yourselves, it is the gift of God …' (v.8)*

It is impossible for us to get into the kingdom by
human effort. God has to bring us into His kingdom,
and the only condition is that we recognise our need to
reach out to Him because we can do nothing to save
ourselves. Proud people often find it difficult to exercise
the humility needed to get into the kingdom. They want
to contribute something or engage in works of penance
so that they feel involved in the transaction. But, as our
text for today tells us so clearly, 'It is by grace you have
been saved, through faith – and this not from yourselves,
it is the gift of God.' Take it from me, there is no one in
the kingdom of God who is not poor in spirit. If they
weren't, they just wouldn't be there.

*Father, it is only empty hands that can receive Christ. I
have nothing to give but I have everything to receive. I am
a candidate for the kingdom. Amen.*

A description of character

FOR READING AND MEDITATION
ISAIAH 61:1–11

*'The Spirit of the Sovereign LORD is on me, because the
Lord has anointed me ... to comfort all who mourn ...'*
(vv. 1–2)

We come to the second of Jesus' sayings: 'Blessed
are those who mourn, for they will be comforted'
(Matt. 5:4). Our Lord does not present the Beatitudes
in a random manner; every one, I believe, was carefully
and prayerfully thought through by our Lord and given
a precise place in the spiritual sequence. Once we
see that entrance into the kingdom of God is through
the acknowledgment of our spiritual poverty and the
acceptance of Christ's resources then we are ready to go
on and consider the next Beatitude. First we must know
the Person – Jesus. Then, when we know Him deeply
and intimately, we will find these qualities appearing in
our lives as naturally and as easily as a flower opens up
to the sun.

*Father, I am so thankful that the Christian life is not my
responsibility, but my response to Your ability. Amen.*

Facing reality

FOR READING AND MEDITATION
ROMANS 8:28–39

'... in all things God works for the good of those who love him, who have been called according to his purpose.' (v.28)

The second Beatitude, 'Blessed are those who mourn, for they will be comforted' (Matt. 5:4), seems somewhat strange and difficult to understand. Most commentators say that we should mourn over our sin and then find comfort in Christ. But did our Lord have something else in mind as well as this? Life can be painful. An unfaithful spouse lets you down, a child takes drugs, somebody fails to come through for you and so on. Being willing to accept that life is difficult will save us from unrealistic expectations which can trigger stress and even depression. Then, when troubles come, we are not surprised, but face reality in the confidence that no matter what happens to us, God will turn it to good.

O Father, help me be a realist – someone who faces reality in the knowledge that there is nothing to fear when You are near. Amen.

A heart afraid of breaking

FOR READING AND MEDITATION
PSALM 23:1–6

'Even though I walk through the valley of the shadow of death, I will fear no evil, for you are with me …' (v.4)

O swald Chambers said, 'Life is more tragic than orderly.' When we look at life with a realistic gaze we see grim and depressing things happening around us. But if we try to avoid negative feelings, eventually we will not be able to feel positive emotions either to their fullest extent. One good principle of emotional, mental and spiritual health is this: integrity requires that whatever is true must be faced. And here's another: a balanced view of life is essential if we are to live effectively. Some cope by becoming detached and emotionally anaesthetised but instead live in tedium and boredom. In the words of an old song: *It's the heart that's afraid of breaking that never learns to dance.*

Father, help me, I pray, to be willing to face anything that comes – good, bad or indifferent. With You in my heart I need fear nothing. Amen.

Honest to God

FOR READING AND MEDITATION
PSALM 51:1–6

'Surely you desire truth in the inner parts; you teach me wisdom in the inmost place.' (v.6)

We must not be afraid to face the negative emotions that may, from time to time, arise within us. This is the first step in the process of mourning. A woman I counselled whose marriage was a troubled one was afraid to feel any negative emotions. She repressed feelings such as grief, sorrow, sadness or regret, and her claim to always being happy was really a spurious one. It was a happiness achieved by means of denial, which is not the kind of happiness Christ wants us to have. At last she came to see that she was avoiding facing reality. It was a good moment both for her and for me when she came out from behind her defensiveness and was then able to rise to a new level of honesty in her life.

O Father, You long for me to be an honest person; I long for that too. Please help me, dear Father. In Jesus' name. Amen.

'Dumping and stuffing'

FOR READING AND MEDITATION
GALATIANS 5:16–26

*'But the fruit of the Spirit is love, joy, peace, patience ...
gentleness and self-control.' (vv.22–23)*

There are many who do not deny their emotions, but give expression to them in ways that are harmful to the personality or other people. One of the fruits of the Spirit is self-control. The Spirit's purpose is to help us live effectively. When an emotion arises within us which we know is unacceptable we must not pretend it is not there. We must acknowledge it. However, it is important that we do not angrily dump that emotion onto another person. Psychologists call this 'stuffing and dumping'. You do not need to express an emotion to deal with it effectively, but you must acknowledge it. All we have to do is to yield to the Spirit. He will help us keep our emotions in check.

Father, please take my hand as I move through this area and lead me to clear biblical conclusions. Amen.

Mastery of the emotions

FOR READING AND MEDITATION
EPHESIANS 4:17–28

'"In your anger do not sin": Do not let the sun go down while you are still angry …' (v.26)

Whenever we are unwilling to face and feel a negative emotion it implies that we are not in charge of it but that it is in charge of us. Our Lord does not want us to be mastered by our emotions but to draw upon His power so that we remain in the position of mastery. We should pray something like this: 'Lord, right now I am hurting so much I do not think I can endure it. I feel like screaming, running away or even hitting someone. I don't want to feel like this, Lord, but I do. Thank You for loving me as I am. Help me now to handle my feelings in a way that glorifies You and honours Your name.' In this way you have not denied your emotions but have opened them up to the Lord and asked for His help.

O Father, I long not to be mastered by my emotions but to be master over them. Teach me this art. Amen.

Wounded healers

FOR READING AND MEDITATION
2 CORINTHIANS 1:1–11

'Praise be to the God and Father of our Lord Jesus Christ, the Father of compassion and the God of all comfort …' (v.3)

Those who refuse to mourn and pretend they are not hurting when they are make it difficult (perhaps even impossible) for God to pour His comfort into their souls. Their pretence forms a barrier that a God who respects human freedom will not break down. The most productive people on earth are those who have opened themselves up to the Lord with complete honesty, have told Him how hurt they are, and have had the experience of those hurts being healed by His love. They have then become what someone has called 'wounded healers'. Having been healed themselves, they have gone out to heal others. Great sorrow can lead to great happiness when we decide to be real and allow the comfort of God to fully invade us.

Father, may I be willing to accept this second Beatitude and prescription for happiness. Please help me become completely whole and a blessing to others. Amen.

'The fruit of power'

FOR READING AND MEDITATION
PSALM 37:1–11

'But the meek will inherit the land and enjoy great peace.'
(v.11)

The words 'Blessed are the meek' (Matt. 5:5) sound rather odd to our ears tuned as they are to popular theories of success where the aggressive are the ones that get ahead. We tend to think of meek people as weak, mild mannered or timid, but that is not the meaning of the original Greek word. The Greek scholar, W.E. Vine, said, 'It must be clearly understood that the meekness … commended to the believer is the fruit of power.' The truly meek person, in the biblical sense, is not passive or compliant, but confident and secure because he or she trusts in God. The biblically meek are those who have a true view of themselves and of their dependence on God, and are gentle when relating to others.

Gracious Father, help me understand that whatever my nature, I can be changed by the power of Your transforming love. Amen.

Yieldedness and surrender

FOR READING AND MEDITATION
ZEPHANIAH 3:1–12

'But I will leave within you the meek and humble, who trust in the name of the Lord.' (v.12)

The meaning of the word 'meek', as used by Jesus, is that of yieldedness or surrender, freedom from belligerence or aggressiveness. It is a common assumption that when people are described as meek they cannot help themselves. But in biblical terms the meek are aware that they have the infinite resources of God to draw upon every moment of every hour. Meekness is gentleness under the constraint of great power. It takes strength to be meek. Our Lord said: 'Take my yoke upon you and learn from me, for I am gentle [or meek] and humble in heart ...' (Matt. 11:29). The consciousness of power was the secret of His meekness; His meekness was rooted in God. Jesus was great because meek, and meek because great.

Lord Jesus Christ, You who are meek and humble in heart, give me Your mind so that I can follow in Your footsteps. Amen.

Grace – not genes

FOR READING AND MEDITATION
COLOSSIANS 3:1–17

'... as God's chosen people ... clothe yourselves with
compassion, kindness, humility, gentleness and patience.'
(v.12)

When we follow Jesus Christ we have access to
a power that can bring about great changes in
our personalities. All Christians, without exception,
should possess this attitude of meekness. In order
to be completely sure what meekness is, it might be
helpful to look first at what it is not. Meekness is not
indolence. There are some people who might appear
to have the quality of meekness but really what they
have is indolence, which is an aversion to exertion. The
meekness our Lord wants us to possess is not something
that arises from our own nature or temperament but is
a gift that comes down from above. It is not a matter of
genes; it is a matter of grace.

*Loving heavenly Father, please transform me day by day
into the person You want me to be. In Jesus' name. Amen.*

'Anything for a quiet life'

FOR READING AND MEDITATION
I PETER 3:1–12

*'Your beauty ... should be that of your inner self, the
unfading beauty of a gentle and quiet spirit ...' (vv.3–4)*

M eekness is not just being easy-going or laid back
– the attitude seen in those who just take life as
it comes. We must learn to differentiate between that
which is natural and that which is spiritual. When I asked
one man to sum up his attitude to life he thought for a
moment and then said, 'Anything for a quiet life.' That is
not meekness, that is weakness. The meek accept God's
demands, and in His name confront issues, refusing to
compromise. They will not allow things to be swept
under the carpet simply to avoid unpleasantness. The
truly meek person is strong enough to confront anything
that is not in accordance with God's will, and is given
the resources of God to do so.

*Heavenly Father, whatever my natural temperament,
please work in my life so that I grow in meekness. In Jesus'
name. Amen.*

All things serve

FOR READING AND MEDITATION
TITUS 3:1–11

'Remind the people … to show true humility towards all men.' (vv.1–2)

The meek are free from a spirit of demandingness – the attitude of those who assert that everything should go their way, or that they ought to be given more consideration, or that people should respect their rights. Christians who are meek will not be oversensitive about themselves, nor defensive, for they are content to leave everything in the hands of God, trusting Him to keep His promise that every negative will be turned to a positive, and every difficulty become a door of opportunity. Robert Browning wrote, 'He who keeps one end in view makes all things serve.' When that one end is confidence in the plans of God for our life, and His power to make what He desires happen, then indeed all things serve.

O God let there not be in me a spirit of demandingness but rather a willingness to trust You in all things. Amen.

What is real strength?

FOR READING AND MEDITATION
I TIMOTHY 6:11–21

'... *pursue righteousness, godliness, faith, love, endurance and gentleness.*' (v.11)

R.B. Jones said that 'Blessed are the meek' could be paraphrased: 'Blessed are those who remain strong, calm and assured in the midst of life's most difficult circumstances.' Think of it. What is real strength? Who is the stronger: the young man who gives in to his rage and becomes physically or verbally abusive or the young man who remains calm, patient and composed? The meek are those who know how to use their power wisely; their strength lies in self-control and discipline. They remain gentle in their relationships with others and don't suffer from a know-it-all attitude. They allow room in their lives for growth. They listen; they are not defensive; they are not on an ego trip but a spiritual journey.

My Father and my God, help me I pray to be an assured being – someone who is so sure of You that I become more sure of myself. Amen.

Judging the world

FOR READING AND MEDITATION
I CORINTHIANS 6:1–11

'Do you not know that the saints will judge the world?' (v.2)

Ultimately meekness is displayed by those who are reliant upon God and have a right and balanced estimate of themselves. Jesus said meek people 'will inherit the earth'. What does that mean, I wonder? I think it means the universe is behind us in everything we do. It works with us. The universe is an orderly one; the sun never crashes into the moon or vice versa. The meek find themselves following an orderly path, just as the universe does, and are as balanced as the universe is balanced. Also some commentators think Jesus' mention of the meek inheriting the earth may have a future reference because in the verse that is our text for today we are told the saints will judge the world.

O Father, deepen within me this sense of meekness so that I stand tall and strong in the midst of life's circumstances. Amen.

Satisfaction – a by-product

FOR READING AND MEDITATION
2 TIMOTHY 2:14–26

'Flee the evil desires of youth, and pursue righteousness …'
(v.22)

Jesus said: 'Blessed are those who hunger and thirst for righteousness, for they will be filled' (Matt. 5:6). Those who seek to be blessed or reach out for satisfaction remain unsatisfied. Satisfaction and contentment, we must understand, are by-products. We do not find them; they find us. If we make gaining contentment, blessedness or satisfaction a goal, then it will elude us like a will-o'-the-wisp. However, if we give up the chase and focus on living in a right relationship with God, then blessedness will take up residence in our hearts. Our primary concern should always be to put the Lord and His righteousness first. When we get taken up with His righteousness He, in return, gives us satisfaction.

O Father, help me, I pray, to have the right priorities in my life. May I be more taken up with knowing You and loving You than with anything else. Amen.

What is righteousness?

FOR READING AND MEDITATION
PROVERBS 8:1–21

'I walk in the way of righteousness, along the paths of justice …' (v.20)

Wat is this righteousness of which our Lord speaks in the Beatitudes? The word 'righteousness' can also be translated 'justice'. Here, however, I think it means much more than that. The desire for righteousness – the act of hungering and thirsting for it – is a longing to be as free from sin as possible and to be in a right relationship with God. In other words, it is responding to all that is right and good and true as laid out for us in the Scriptures. When we commit ourselves to righteousness, and are quick to repent when sin enters our lives, then we move forward even though we may never achieve absolute holiness and perfection here on earth. This is how we grow.

O Lord, I long to be a righteous person – someone who lives according to the Scriptures, never excusing my sin but always being ready to repent of it. Amen.

Starving for God

FOR READING AND MEDITATION
PSALM 42:1–11

'As the deer pants for streams of water, so my soul pants for you, O God.' (v.1)

Our Lord, when using the phrase 'hunger and thirst', chose His words carefully. The feelings of hunger and thirst are not ones that are fleeting; they do not just disappear but go on increasing until one is satisfied with food and drink. They can make one feel desperate and even cause great pain. In my opinion the psalmist sums up the matter perfectly when he writes, 'As the deer pants for streams of water, so my soul pants for you, O God.' The commentator J.N. Darby, wrote, 'To be hungry and thirsty is not enough; we must really be *starving* [emphasis mine] to know what is in His heart toward us. When the prodigal son was hungry he went to feed upon husks, but when he was starving he turned to his father.'

O God, I am desperate to know You better in a deeper and more intimate relationship with You than I have ever experienced before. Amen.

Three simple tests

FOR READING AND MEDITATION
HEBREWS 11:1–13

'Now faith is being sure of what we hope for ... This is what the ancients were commended for.' (vv.1–2)

L et me suggest a few checks to tell if we are hungering and thirsting for righteousness. The first is to ask if we can see the total inadequacy of our own false righteousness (Isa. 64:6). The second is to ask ourselves if we have a real awareness of our need of a Saviour. Do we recognise our complete inability to save ourselves and understand that if God had not sent His Son to save us then we would have been lost forever? A third test is this: when we read about Bible characters who were out and out for God, such as the men and women we have read about in Hebrews 11, do we find ourselves longing to be like them? Can you pass these tests?

Gracious and most merciful heavenly Father, I long to have a heart that hungers and thirsts for righteousness. To You I yield my all this day. Amen.

Staying spiritually hungry

FOR READING AND MEDITATION
ISAIAH 55:1–13

'Come, all you who are thirsty … Listen, listen to me, and eat what is good …' (vv.1–2)

A person who hungers and thirsts for righteousness is not content with avoiding those things that have the appearance of unrighteousness – the things that are bad and harmful. They also avoid those things that may be harmless and legitimate yet take the edge off their spiritual appetite. It would be difficult to condemn many of the things that occupy our attention in life, but if we spend too much time with them we will want spiritual things less and less. All of us know how in the physical realm it is easy to spoil our appetite – by eating between meals, for example. Similarly, we must take great care that in the spiritual realm we do not indulge in anything that affects our hunger and thirst for God.

Father, may I be careful and prayerful about my spiritual appetite, and guide me so that I do not do anything to spoil that appetite. Amen.

The daily quiet time

FOR READING AND MEDITATION
ISAIAH 64:1–12

'... no eye has seen any God besides you, who acts on behalf of those who wait for him.' (v.4)

Hungry and thirsty people want to meet God through prayer and the reading of His Word on a daily, or certainly regular, basis. Those who do not pray and read the Bible regularly will very quickly lose their appetite for the things of God. Everyone needs to develop their own approach to what used to be called 'the quiet time'. I suggest you set aside a particular part of the day, and spend time alone with God. Anyone who argues that they can pray at any time and fails to have a fixed time of prayer is likely to end up praying none of the time. Some may say they do not have the time, but if you are really hungering and thirsting for righteousness then you will make the effort to find the time.

O Father, I realise that hungering and thirsting for You involves taking certain steps. May I actively pursue righteousness. In Jesus' name. Amen.

Blessed paradox

FOR READING AND MEDITATION
PHILIPPIANS 3:1–11

'I want to know Christ and the power of his resurrection …'
(v.10)

Those who hunger and thirst for righteousness will 'be filled' (Matt. 5:6). One commentator says that growing Christians are those who hunger and thirst for God and are filled, yet the more they are filled the more they hunger and thirst. Blessed paradox. We continually go on 'being transformed into [Christ's] likeness with ever-increasing glory' (2 Cor. 3:18). Can you say honestly and truly that your desire above everything else in the world is to really know God and be like the Lord Jesus Christ, to be rid of self-centredness and sin in every shape and form, and to live only for His glory and His honour? Then you can rest assured that you are someone who hungers and thirsts for righteousness.

Father, the more of You I have the more I long for. Constantly sharpen my spiritual appetite I pray. In Jesus' name. Amen.

It's good for us

FOR READING AND MEDITATION
LUKE 6:27–36

'Be merciful, just as your Father is merciful.' (v.36)

We come now to a fifth attitude we must adopt if we are to experience a soul that is contented: 'Blessed are the merciful, for they will be shown mercy' (Matt. 5:7). The blessed life is one in which the quality of mercy is always present. The unblessed life is one in which the heart is filled with thoughts of vengeance, retaliation and the settling of scores. Probably more times than we'll ever know, the unhappiness of those who choose the way of vengeance is increased through the breakdown of their physical health – through high blood pressure, heart trouble or strokes produced by stress. There is, however, an alternative that we can choose – the positive attitude of being merciful and forgiving.

O God, let the quality of mercy always be present in me I pray. In Jesus' name. Amen.

A spiritual disposition

FOR READING AND MEDITATION
JOHN 15:1–17

'If anyone does not remain in me, he is like a branch that is thrown away and withers …' (v.6)

There are those who live in hate with constant thoughts of vengeance and retaliation in their minds, but all that their spite and spleen accomplishes is the ultimate devouring of themselves. The people who are blessed are those with a disposition that is merciful. I am not talking now about a natural disposition but a spiritual one. No Christian can get away with saying, 'It isn't in my nature to be merciful and forgiving.' As one commentator puts it, 'This is not a gospel for certain temperaments – nobody has an advantage over anybody when they are face to face with God.' The disposition to be merciful and forgiving develops within us to the degree that we walk hand in hand with the Master.

Lord Jesus Christ, I see again that I cannot live against You without harming my own life, for life works Your way and no other way. Amen.

Right attitudes: right actions

FOR READING AND MEDITATION
LUKE 23:32–43

'Jesus said, "Father, forgive them, for they do not know what they are doing."' (v.34)

The closer we get to Christ the more His merciful nature is imparted to us by the Holy Spirit. We find ourselves having the same merciful attitude towards others that He has, and from the right attitude flows the right actions. Scripture puts a greater emphasis on our attitudes than our actions. Being precedes doing, and our attitudes precede our actions. When we have the right attitudes then it follows as the night follows the day that our actions will also be right. So don't think that having a merciful disposition is something we gain through a powerful exertion of our will; rather, it is something that flows from Christ to us as a result of our relationship with Him, and then from us to others.

Merciful and wonderful Saviour, transform me so that I become like You I pray. I cannot be a truly merciful person without Your help. Amen.

Mercy and truth – together

'For the LORD your God is a merciful God ...' (v.31)

W.E. Vine says that a merciful person is not simply possessed of pity but is actively compassionate. To fully understand mercy we must take note of the fact that God Himself is merciful. So whatever we decide about mercy we must keep in mind it applies also to God. This means that a laissez faire attitude towards sin is completely out of the question, for God is not only merciful but righteous and holy and just. As the prophet Habakkuk tells us, He 'cannot tolerate wrong' (Hab. 1:13). 'Mercy and truth are met together,' says the psalmist in Psalm 85:10 (AV). So if we think of mercy at the expense of truth and law we will have a false understanding of what is involved in being merciful.

O God, save me from becoming a lop-sided Christian – someone who holds to one truth but not another. May mercy and truth meet also in me. Amen.

Compassion plus action

FOR READING AND MEDITATION
LUKE 10:25–37

'But a Samaritan ... took pity on him. He went to him and bandaged his wounds ...' (vv.33–34)

One of the best ways to understand 'mercy' is to compare it with 'grace'. While grace looks down upon sin and seeks to save, mercy looks especially upon the miserable consequences of sin and seeks to relieve. A Christian who demonstrates mercy will not only feel compassion for someone, but will not be content until they have done something about the plight of the one with whom they have come in contact. The story of the Good Samaritan, which we have read today, is a classic illustration of how to be merciful. Others saw but did nothing. The Samaritan took the badly injured man to an inn and made provision for his comfort. Mercy is compassion plus action.

Gracious, loving and merciful Lord, help me not only to understand mercy but to put it into action in my life. Amen.

Am I a merciful person?

FOR READING AND MEDITATION
HEBREWS 4:12–16

*'Let us then approach the throne of grace with confidence,
so that we may receive mercy ...' (v.16)*

We must ask ourselves: Am I a merciful person?
This is one way in which you can tell whether
you are, or are not, a merciful person: when you are in a
position of power over someone who has harmed you,
do you find you enjoy the feeling that you can exact a
penalty from them? Do you say to yourself, 'This person
has wronged me and treated me badly – now I have the
opportunity to retaliate'? That is the very opposite of
being merciful. If, however, when a person has treated
you unjustly there is in your heart a feeling of being hurt
but no desire to hurt back – no feeling of contempt or
scorn for the person concerned – then you are a truly
merciful person.

*O God, slowly but surely I am coming under the sway of
Your beautiful attitudes. For that I am eternally grateful.
Amen.*

I'm forgiven

FOR READING AND MEDITATION
EPHESIANS 4:29–5:2

'Be kind and compassionate to one another, forgiving each other …' (v.32)

Our salvation depends on our repentance, and when we repent then our sins are forgiven and we are guaranteed a place in heaven. If, after we are forgiven, we refuse to give forgiveness to others it does not mean we lose our salvation, but it does make it difficult, or even impossible, for God's forgiveness to reach the very core of our lives. This is why there are many who do not have a realised sense of God's forgiveness. They have been forgiven, but the full wonder of God's forgiveness cannot penetrate the depths of their being. The act of forgiving makes us more able to receive. When we express mercy and forgiveness to others we also experience it deep down in our own hearts and lives.

Heavenly Father, when resentment rises please help me to quench it with the support of Your Holy Spirit. Amen.

Spiritual heart surgery

FOR READING AND MEDITATION
MATTHEW 15:1–20

'But the things that come out of the mouth come from the heart, and these make a man "unclean".' (v.18)

The sixth saying of Jesus, to which we now turn our attention is this: 'Blessed are the pure in heart, for they will see God' (Matt. 5:8). The heart is more than just the seat of the affections; it is the fount from which everything proceeds. The good news is a gospel of *new* things. It offers men and women a *new* birth, a *new* life, a *new* hope, a *new* happiness, and one day, when we arrive in heaven, a *new* name. In Ezekiel 36:26 God also promises: 'I will give you a new heart and put a new spirit in you.' When it comes to spiritual matters, the heart of the matter is the matter of the heart. God is not content to change our outward behaviour. His goal is to purify our hearts, and we must yield our all to Him until that is accomplished.

Lord Jesus Christ, You whose heart was totally pure, please make my heart like Your own. Amen.

Purity and power

FOR READING AND MEDITATION
ACTS 15:1–11

'He made no distinction between us and them, for he purified their hearts by faith.' (v.9)

What did Jesus mean when He said, 'Blessed are the *pure* in heart, for they will see God' (Matt. 5:8)? The Greek word *katharos*, which is translated 'pure', means cleansed, and so conveys a heart that is clean or clear. One of the greatest challenges we face as Christians is the challenge to experience purity of heart, but in many Christian circles today the word 'purity' does not sit well with people. The emphasis nowadays seems to be more on power than on purity. Many of the Christians I meet and talk to want to know how they can get more spiritual power in their lives. Although that is a legitimate desire, I think God wants us to be as keen on purity as we are on power.

Yes, my Father, give me a clear heart I pray. I have come so far with You, and don't want to turn back now. I long not only for power but also for purity. Cleanse me and make me whole. Amen.

As white as snow

FOR READING AND MEDITATION
PSALM 51:7–19

'Cleanse me with hyssop, and I shall be clean; wash me,
and I shall be whiter than snow.' (v.7)

Three views of purity can be presented: (1) those who
believe that purity is imputed; (2) those who believed
that purity is imparted, and (3) those who believe that
purity is developed. The first believe Christ flings His robe
of righteousness around a sinner at the time of his or
her conversion, and then God sees that person dressed
in the spotless garments of His Son. Those who believe
purity is imparted maintain that some time after their
conversion God imparts to believers the gift of purity,
usually through a crisis experience. Those who believe
purity is developed see the work of God as proceeding
along the lines of a slow but steady improvement. I
believe each view has something to contribute.

Father, I am so thankful You provide for all my needs,
especially my need for inner cleansing. Wash me so that I
shall be whiter than snow. Amen.

'Lord, make me clean'

FOR READING AND MEDITATION
ROMANS 7:14–8:4

'… through Christ Jesus the law of the Spirit of life set me free from the law of sin and death.' (8:2)

After my conversion, I still felt troubled by the sinful forces which continued to stir deep within me. I fought hard with such matters as lust and sensuality until one day I fell to my knees and cried, 'Lord, reach deep inside me and make me truly clean.' Something wonderful happened. My inner being was invaded with purity. This did not place me beyond the possibility of a carnal thought, a stab of pride, a trace of envy, but it meant that I was more conscious of the Holy Spirit's presence than I was of sin's presence. Sin was not entirely eradicated in me, but I found the eagerness for it had gone and the hunger for it no longer a clamour. God imputed, imparted and developed purity in me.

O Father, whatever work needs to be done in my soul, I hold nothing back. Above all things I long to have a heart that is pure. Amen.

No divisions

FOR READING AND MEDITATION
HEBREWS 10:19–39

'... let us draw near to God with a sincere heart in full
assurance of faith ...' (v.22)

Commentators generally agree that a pure heart
consists of two things: single-mindedness and
freedom from defilement. One of our greatest problems
as Christians is that frequently our hearts are divided;
one part of us wants to know God and another part of
us wants something else. The pure heart is a heart that
is undivided; it seeks to draw close to God and makes
Him its chief goal. In Psalm 86:11 the psalmist pleads,
'... give me an undivided heart, that I may fear your
name.' However, that is not the only thought behind
the word 'pure'; it obviously carries the meaning of
cleansing also. These two things then – singleness of
mind and freedom from defilement – are necessary if we
are to see God.

O Father, the more I think of what it means to have a pure
heart, the more I find myself longing for one. In Jesus' name.
Amen.

Seeing God

FOR READING AND MEDITATION
PSALM 24:1–10

'Who may ascend the hill of the LORD? … He who has clean hands and a pure heart …' (vv.3–4)

In my opinion, Jesus had in mind not just seeing God when we get to heaven but seeing Him in the here and now. Christians see God in a way no one else can. They see Him in nature, in the events of history, in their daily experiences, in the pages of the Bible, and so on. Seeing God is being acquainted with Him, sensing His acceptance, comprehending what it means to be forgiven and made anew. Raymond Cramer puts it beautifully when he says, 'To the pure in heart seeing God is like viewing a stained-glass window from the inside rather than the outside.' Seeing God is inextricably linked with purity of heart. It cannot be otherwise.

O Father, how I long to be able to see You. Please purify my heart so that I might have a clear vision of You and thus reflect Your glory. Amen.

Catharsis

FOR READING AND MEDITATION
ISAIAH 9:1–7

'And he will be called Wonderful Counsellor ...' (v.6)

'Catharsis' means to make clean, and is derived from the same Greek root as the word 'pure'. In psychology the word 'catharsis' is used to describe the sense of cleansing a person experiences in the presence of a trusted friend or counsellor, when they empty out feelings or ideas that have been repressed. In the right circumstances and under the right conditions a person who does this feels released and renewed. Catharsis happens only in an atmosphere of mutual trust with the one doing the listening being a non-judgmental person. In Christ we have a Counsellor who, when we open up our hearts to Him, can help us experience the deepest catharsis it is possible to know.

Father, Son and Holy Spirit, take me deeper into You I pray. May I know a deep catharsis in my soul this very day. In Jesus' name. Amen.

The peace of God

FOR READING AND MEDITATION
ROMANS 5:1–11

'Therefore, since we have been justified through faith, we have peace with God through our Lord Jesus Christ ...' (v.1)

The seventh of our Lord's famous sayings is: 'Blessed are the peacemakers, for they will be called sons of God' (Matt. 5:9). Peace movements are reporting increasing support, yet the other side of the coin is this: large numbers of those who press for peace between nations fail to see the need for peace between themselves and God. A friend of mine who at one time was very prominent in a peace movement told me that during the years he was active and was meeting with politicians and other key people to press for peace, he knew no real peace in his heart. Then one day he found Christ, and in finding peace with God he also found the peace of God.

My Father, thank You for the peace that You have put within my own heart. How I praise You that this peace is a peace that never goes to pieces. Amen.

Repairing the breach

FOR READING AND MEDITATION
HEBREWS 12:1–14

'Make every effort to live in peace with all men and to be holy ...' (v.14)

O n the day I was ordained I opened up my Bible to receive a word from God, and my eyes alighted on this verse: '... thou shalt be called, The repairer of the breach, The restorer of paths to dwell in' (Isa. 58:12, AV). Being a peacemaker can be hazardous, especially when you are attempting to bring about a reconciliation and the opposing sides end up turning on you. But it's necessary to take that risk if breaches are to be repaired. Almost everyone can be a peacemaker. The mother who helps resolve the arguments and disturbances that take place in the family is such a person. Stay alert. God may use you as a peacemaker this very day.

My Father and my God, help me not to miss opportunities to be a peacemaker. In Jesus' name. Amen.

The Prince of Peace

FOR READING AND MEDITATION
ISAIAH 9:1–7

'And he will be called … Prince of Peace.' (v.6)

Of all the Messiah's titles, the one I find most captivating is 'Prince of Peace'. The apostle Paul in his letter to the Philippians tells us that Christ left His home in glory in order to enter this strife-torn planet and reconcile humankind to God, to bridge the gulf that existed between us and God. There is no greater truth to be found anywhere in the Bible than the truth that Jesus Christ came to end the hostility between ourselves and God and bring peace to the troubled hearts of humanity. With Christ's love within us we can follow in His footsteps by helping to reconcile those whose relationships are wrecked and broken. Don't let any broken relationships in your family or church remain that way. It is dishonouring to the Prince of Peace.

Blessed Lord and Master, Prince of Peace, teach me the art of peacemaking I pray. Amen.

Peace in our hearts

FOR READING AND MEDITATION
JAMES 3:1–18

'Peacemakers who sow in peace raise a harvest of righteousness.' (v.18)

Those who seek to be peacemakers will be more effective when they ensure there are no unresolved conflicts within themselves. The simple truth is that often when we lose our peace with others we are projecting an inner conflict we ourselves have. Usually those who constantly run out of patience with their families or the people with whom they work are out of patience with themselves. On entering a church in the Far East I saw this sign: 'Let every Christian begin the work of union within their own self.' This is the place to begin – with yourself. Those who have peace in their own hearts are able to share that with others. When we are truly at peace with God we are at peace with ourselves.

Heavenly Father, once more I thank You from the depths of my being that I have found in You a peace that nothing can destroy. Amen.

Peacemaking is not easy

FOR READING AND MEDITATION
I CORINTHIANS 16:5–18

'Be on your guard; stand firm in the faith; be men of courage; be strong.' (v.13)

Being a peacemaker involves more than just keeping the peace. Some strive to keep the peace simply in order to avoid unpleasantness. They avoid a conflict by dealing with superficial problems but don't get down to the real issues. Paradoxically, a peacemaker is called not to a passive role but an active one. At times a peacemaker has to be a fighter. Those who settle for peace at any price will find that the peace they think they have achieved will eventually fall to pieces. Peacemaking is not a matter of patching things up but of getting to the roots of a problem. All this, of course, requires courage – the courage to risk making mistakes. Peacemaking is not easy, but then nothing worthwhile is.

O God, make me a courageous person, especially when I am called to intervene between people who have been offended. Amen.

'Outer obnoxiousness'

FOR READING AND MEDITATION
ROMANS 14:13–23

'Let us therefore make every effort to do what leads to peace and to mutual edification.' (v.19)

Relational peace comes when the truth is faced, issues are settled, and the warring parties embrace one another. Peacemakers are active makers of peace; they go out of their way to reconcile. They use their influence to end party strife and bring together those opposed to one another. I remember a Peanuts cartoon in which Lucy explodes in a fit of temper and shouts, 'I hate everything. I hate everybody. I hate the whole wide world.' Charlie Brown retorts, 'But I thought you had inner peace.' In reply Lucy explains, 'Yes, but I also have outer obnoxiousness.' Inner peace and outer obnoxiousness cancel one another out. It is not the Christian way.

Father, help me to be a peacemaker, not just a peacekeeper. In Jesus' name. Amen.

Three types of people

FOR READING AND MEDITATION
PSALM 34:1–22

'Turn from evil and do good; seek peace and pursue it.'
(v.14)

I have noticed that when it comes to the matter of peace there are three types of people – peacebreakers, peacefakers and peacemakers. Peacebreakers are those who say the wrong things, do the wrong things, confront, disagree and cause divisions. Peacefakers are those who prefer peace to truth. They regard peace simply as the absence of any kind of argument or discord. Although they give the impression they are for peace, in reality what they are for is avoiding troubled waters. Peacemakers, however, are those who are equally committed to peace and truth, and are prepared to be misjudged or hurt in their pursuit of bringing together those whose relationships need to be reconciled or re-established.

Father, I want not merely to have the name of a peacemaker, I want to be one. In Jesus' name I pray. Amen.

Not once, but twice

FOR READING AND MEDITATION
ACTS 16:16–40

'About midnight Paul and Silas were praying and singing hymns to God ...' (v.25)

The last of Christ's prescriptions for the life that is blessed is: 'Blessed are those who are persecuted ... Blessed ... when people ... persecute you ...' Jesus doesn't say once that the persecuted are blessed; He says it twice. This Beatitude is a paradox. How can the persecuted be blessed? Most of us feel bad if we have a stressful day, let alone if we face persecution. How different it was with the apostle Paul and his companion Silas. These two intrepid warriors apparently remembered Jesus' instruction, 'Rejoice and be glad' (Matt. 5:12). Years later Paul would write to the church in Philippi from another prison – this time in Rome – and tell them, 'Rejoice in the Lord always. I will say it again: Rejoice!' (Phil. 4:4).

O God, help me rejoice even in the midst of persecution – with all the stops out! In Jesus' name. Amen.

'The sight of your own blood'

FOR READING AND MEDITATION
LUKE 6:17–26

'Woe to you when all men speak well of you ...' (v.26)

J esus warns that if people speak well of us it could
be that we are too much like them. The teaching
of Scripture is that once we adopt the attitudes and
principles which Christ presents so clearly for us in His
Sermon on the Mount then some men and women of the
world are going to react with hostility, indignation and
persecution. One pastor known to me tells the converts
in his church, 'The first thing you must get used to is the
sight of your own blood – metaphorically speaking, of
course.' Are you experiencing some form of persecution
at the moment because of your stand for righteousness?
Then take heart; a limitless supply of grace is flowing
towards you.

*Father, help me to respond to people with patience,
understanding, and above all, love. In Jesus' name.
Amen.*

No hidden agenda

FOR READING AND MEDITATION
JOHN 15:18–27

'If the world hates you, keep in mind that it hated me first.' (v.18)

How thankful we should be that Jesus did not hide anything from us. The point our Lord wants us to remember is that when we are persecuted because of righteousness, the hostility we experience is really not about us but about Him. A Christian should be quite different from those who are not believers – those living according to the culture of the world. *The Message* paraphrases John 15:18: 'If you find the godless world is hating you, remember it got its start hating me.' I like, too, the paraphrase of Matthew 5:10: 'You're blessed when your commitment to God provokes persecution. The persecution drives you even deeper into God's kingdom.' That is something about which we can rejoice.

Lord Jesus Christ, you suffered persecution, yet by Your love and goodwill You returned them as forgiving grace. Help me, I pray, to do the same. Amen.

What persecution is not

FOR READING AND MEDITATION
PSALM 119:153–160

'Many are the foes who persecute me, but I have not turned from your statutes.' (v.157)

F rancis Schaeffer pointed out that if the world does not have a problem with us then we should take that as a warning sign that we may not be conforming to Christ. But in trying to understand persecution, let's not make the mistake of thinking of ourselves as being persecuted because of righteousness when we are not. When a person questions our beliefs, for example, this is not persecution. Having someone disagree with us is not persecution. A conflict between you and an unbeliever, however sharp the dispute, is not necessarily persecution. Persecution is a malicious attack upon someone because of their testimony and faith in Jesus Christ.

Gracious Father, shine Your Holy Spirit into my heart so that I might see if my life is being lived in correspondence with Your Word. Amen.

The freedom to choose

FOR READING AND MEDITATION
2 CORINTHIANS 12:1–10

*'My grace is sufficient for you, for my power is made
perfect in weakness.' (v.9)*

You may know the story of the renowned Austrian
psychiatrist, Dr Victor Frankl, a Jew imprisoned
by the Nazis in four concentration camps, including
Auschwitz, in World War II, and author of the book
Man's Search for Meaning. The Gestapo forced Victor
to strip. But they noticed that he was still wearing his
wedding ring, and they took that from him. As they did,
he said to himself, 'You can take away my wife and my
children. You can strip me of my clothes and my freedom,
but there is one thing no one can ever take from me –
and that is my freedom to choose how I will react to
what happens to me.' As Christians we have freedom to
choose to respond with God's love and grace.

*O God, give me strength and courage to stand my ground,
and wisdom, too, so that I may handle all situations with
creativity and love. Amen.*

Don't cultivate eccentricity

FOR READING AND MEDITATION
COLOSSIANS 4:1–6

'Be wise in the way you act towards outsiders; make the most of every opportunity.' (v.5)

S ome people in society think that when a person becomes a Christian he or she has gone mad. I once heard about a young woman who gave up her job as a barmaid when she was converted. Her friends thought she had lost her senses. They treated her as if she were mad and completely ostracised her. There is a shame at the heart of the cross and it must be borne. Yet even though we should expect to bear disgrace and reproach for the cause of Christ, we must be careful that we do not increase that reproach by our eccentricities. Sadly, some Christians seem to cultivate eccentricity and act in ways that are foolish and unnecessary. Christ came to save and sanctify us, not to make us eccentrics.

Gracious Father, save me from any eccentric or foolish ways as I relate to my family, my friends and those with whom I come in contact in my daily life. Amen.

Bearing His reproach

FOR READING AND MEDITATION
HEBREWS 13:1–13

*'Let us, then, go to him outside the camp, bearing the
disgrace he bore.' (v.13)*

Hebrews, addressing a suffering people who had
endured persecution says: 'Let us, then, go to him
outside the camp.' It is as if he is asking us not to allow
ourselves to be dragged to the place of rejection but to go
willingly, to thrust our shoulders under the cross and say
that since Christ has borne so much for us, we will gladly
bear this for Him. Whenever you are reproached because
of the gospel tell yourself, 'This is not my reproach. It is
His. This is the shame of Jesus, crucified on a cross – and
I am being allowed to experience something of what He
suffered.' And when, for Christ's sake, you are made an
object of reviling, 'Rejoice and be glad, because great is
your reward in heaven' (Matt. 5:12).

*Thank You, my Father, for all You have brought to my heart.
Now let my new attitudes allow me to reach new spiritual
altitudes. Amen.*

Can we trust the Bible?

FOR READING AND MEDITATION
JOHN 10:22–42

'... the Scripture cannot be broken ...' (v.35)

Over the years a number of beliefs – all them of based on the truth found in the Bible – have deepened and become firm convictions. As I look back over my life I realise that I no longer simply hold them – they hold me. The first of the 12 convictions I would like to share with you is this: the Bible is true and absolutely trustworthy. Though I have never been able to answer every question put to me about the Bible that makes no difference to my acceptance of it as the very Word of God. Other books have to be understood before they can be accepted. The Bible has to be accepted before it can be understood. It yields its secrets only to those who come to it believingly.

O God, help me grasp the fact that the words the Bible contains have been breathed into by Your Spirit and have become Your Word. Amen.

How do we get our orders?

FOR READING AND MEDITATION
2 PETER 1:12–21

'… men spoke from God as they were carried along by the Holy Spirit.' (v.21)

There are many in the Church who do not share my conviction that the Bible is the Word of God. They believe it to be an inspirational book, but not necessarily a divinely inspired book. R.C. Sproul asked one such person, 'If you believe Jesus to be your Saviour and your Lord but you do not believe the Bible to be God's Word then how do you get your marching orders … from whom do you get your commands?' The man was nonplussed – and rightly so. If we cannot trust what the Holy Spirit has recorded for us in Scripture then what is our framework of reference? Where do we get our instructions? Without trust in the Bible the Christian life is a daily grind. With trust in the Bible there is daily growth.

O God, I see that You have not only called me to follow You but have given me a route map to guide me. Amen.

Deep, dark, mysterious

FOR READING AND MEDITATION
I CORINTHIANS 2:6–16

*'... the things that come from the Spirit of God ...
are spiritually discerned.' (v.14)*

A writer tells of being present at a magnificent *son et lumiere* at the Palace of Versailles, near Paris. He stood with others outside the building, which was in complete darkness. Then, in one room after another, lights were switched on as over loudspeakers a commentator told the history of the palace. Eventually every window was illuminated and the whole building ablaze with light. This gives us some idea of what happens when we come to the Bible depending on the help and illumination of the Holy Spirit. He turns on the lights in chapter after chapter, book after book. How dark the Word of God would be if it wasn't for the Holy Spirit's enlightening ministry.

Father, I see that without the Holy Spirit's illumination the Bible cannot be properly understood. It remains deep, dark and mysterious. Amen.

Skills without the Spirit

FOR READING AND MEDITATION
2 TIMOTHY 3:1–17

'All Scripture is God-breathed ...' (v.16)

Nothing, in my opinion, can be more sad than listening to someone trying to explain the Bible without depending on the Holy Spirit. Expository skills, taught in Bible colleges, are helpful and necessary, but much more than skills is needed if the message of the Bible is to be made clear. As it is easy to be misunderstood, let me at this point emphasise once again that I am not against skills. I am simply saying that skills without the direction of the Spirit get us nowhere. I have noticed that people who de-emphasise the work of the Spirit in illuminating the Word, and emphasise only critical skills, turn out to be Bible tearers rather than Bible teachers.

O God, how it must hurt You when men and women water down Your Word. Strengthen my conviction that the Bible is Your Word written. Amen.

How to come to the Bible

FOR READING AND MEDITATION
JOB 23:1–17

'… I have treasured the words of his mouth more than my daily bread.' (v.12)

We should come to the Bible believingly. The Bible is not just a good book; it is God's book. We should come to it expectantly. The Bible is alive with meaning. Expect it to speak and it will. We should come to it unhurriedly. If you stride through a forest you will probably see and hear very little, but sit down and you will hear all the sounds of nature because you are quiet and receptive. And we must come to the Bible willing to surrender to the truth it reveals for God is to be obeyed. Finally, we should continue to come to the Bible even if nothing apparently results from it. Just to expose yourself to the Bible is infinitely worthwhile. For where Love is, silence may be the only language.

O God, may Your Word be a lamp to my feet and a light for my path every day of my life. In Christ's name I ask it. Amen.

Blessed obsession!

FOR READING AND MEDITATION
GALATIANS 6:1–18

'May I never boast except in the cross of our Lord Jesus Christ …' (v.14)

The second conviction I hold is this: the cross of our Lord Jesus Christ provides the most profound revelation in the universe. On one occasion I was even accused of being obsessed with it. Blessed obsession! It is here that we see into the depth of things, here the heart of the universe shows itself. A present-day philosopher has written, 'If God exists there is no way that we can understand His essential nature.' Well, God *does* exist, and there *is* a way we can understand His essential nature. The key is the cross. The Almighty has shown Himself willing to sacrifice Himself for others. And nowhere in earth or heaven is self-sacrifice seen in such measure as in the cross.

O Father, it is through the cross and Your Son's redemptive death that I see directly into Your heart. And what I see there sets my heart on fire. Amen.

A sacrificial Head

FOR READING AND MEDITATION
1 JOHN 4:1–12

'… God … loved us and sent his Son as an atoning sacrifice for our sins.' (v.10)

A psychology textbook says: 'The extent of the elevation of an animal, and of course any free moral agent, can be infallibly measured by the degree to which sacrificial love for others controls the being.' Where the sacrificial spirit is absent from life, that life is of the lowest kind. Where it is partially developed, it is slightly higher. Where it is perfectly embodied, that life is highest in the scale of being. If that is a universal law – and it seems to be – then when we come to God, who must represent the highest stage of being, we would expect to find the most highly developed expression of sacrificial love. And that is exactly what we do find. The cross proves it. The universe has a sacrificial Head.

Father God, I see that the highest in humankind is the deepest in You. May this spirit be seen more clearly in me. Amen.

The infallible law

FOR READING AND MEDITATION
GENESIS 18:16–33

'Will not the Judge of all the earth do right?' (v.25)

The spirit of self-sacrifice is built into us. And it is built into us, I believe, by divine design. There is within us a sense of justice – a justice which causes us to feel it is right to save, even at a cost to oneself. If this 'infallible law' of self-sacrifice, as some psychologists describe it, remains true up through the scale of being, but reverses itself when it gets to God, then laws are meaningless and the universe is without a Head. But, on the other hand, if this law holds good from the very lowest to the very highest, as the sacrificial spirit of the cross implies, then the universe is whole, laws are not enigmas, and God is not a disappointment.

Thank You, Father, for showing me that the noblest in human nature points to the noblest expression of Your nature – the cross. Amen.

The nature of love

FOR READING AND MEDITATION
PSALM 94:1–23

'Does he who implanted the ear not hear? Does he who formed the eye not see?' (v.9)

The psalmist points out that it is absurd to think the Creator, who made the human ear and the human eye, cannot hear and cannot see. And, we might add: Does He who implanted within us the spirit of self-sacrifice not have that same spirit Himself? As certainly as God is love, the burdens of being One who loves must fall upon Him, as they do upon us. It is the nature of love universally to place itself into the sorrows and sins of the one it loves and make them its very own. When pure love meets sin or wrongdoing in the one who is loved, a cross of pain is inevitably set up at the point where the two meet. It could not be otherwise, love being what it is: a nature of self-sacrifice.

Father, the more I ponder this the more I feel I am looking into the heart of the greatest thing in this universe of ours – Your love. Amen.

The eternal cross

FOR READING AND MEDITATION
REVELATION 13:1–9

'… the Lamb that was slain from the creation of the world.' (v.8)

Some say that they do not understand what God is like. But the cross lifted up on Calvary was the visible cross through which we see and understand the inner cross in the heart of God. And that cross – Calvary's cross – lights up God's nature and reveals it as being suffering, redemptive love. No greater discovery can be made, or ever will be made, than that. It is the ultimate in discoveries. The cross was not an accident – something read into things by loving hearts; it was the revelation of the heart of the Father. Isn't it to be expected that before our human existence began there has always been an unseen cross in His heart?

Lord Jesus, I see that You carried that cross in Your heart long before it was lifted up on Calvary. For that I shall be forever grateful. Amen.

The Way – unqualified

FOR READING AND MEDITATION
ACTS 9:1–19

'... if he found any there who belonged to the Way,
whether men or women ...' (v.2)

My third conviction is this: God's way is the only
way that works. Jesus talked about two ways: the
way that leads to destruction, and the way that leads to
life (Matt. 7:13–14). But 'the Way' signifies more than
the way of salvation. It encompasses the whole of life
– moral and spiritual. The first Christians were aware of
this, and not only believed something new but behaved
in a manner that was new. Jim Wallis writes, 'Their faith
produced a discernible lifestyle, a way of life ... Christian
belief became identified with a certain kind of behaviour.'
The Way is the Way unqualified. It is the way to do
everything – to think, to feel, to act, to conduct oneself
in every possible circumstance.

*O Father, to live Your way is life – and life abundant. I am
so grateful I have discovered this. Thank You my Father.
Amen.*

The nature of reality

FOR READING AND MEDITATION
JOHN 1:1–18

'Through him all things were made; without him nothing was made ...' (v.3)

God's way is *the* Way, and all other ways are not the way. Is this arrogance? Some might think so, but actually it is the nature of reality. When God, in Christ, made all things, He made them to work in a certain way, and that way is Christ's way. All creation has the stamp of Christ upon it. So the Way is written into the nature of reality as well as into the Scriptures – thus the Way is inescapable for everybody. The Way is not a side issue or a matter for debate. It is the central issue of life – the one issue of life. If you could split open creation you would find imprinted into it like a watermark, 'Made by Him and for Him.' Christ is the Reality by whom all other reality is measured.

O God, I am so thankful that I belong to the Way – inherently. And the Way belongs to me – inherently. Therefore we belong to each other – inherently. Amen.

The great design

FOR READING AND MEDITATION
PROVERBS 14:1–18

'The faithless will be fully repaid for their ways, and the good man rewarded for his.' (v.14)

Can it be that all of life comes down to the fact that there is the Way and not-the-way? Does all of life become a choice between the Way and not-the-way? I am *convinced* it does. That choice confronts us in every thought, in every act, in every feeling, indeed, every time we do anything. As an observer of human life in all its aspects, I am drawn inescapably to the conclusion that God's way is always the right way to do anything, and any other way is always the wrong way. When people live in a manner that goes against the great design, they have to put up with the consequences; when they live in accordance with the great design, they receive its rewards. And there are no exceptions.

Father, I see that life works in one way only – Your way. Help me take that way in everything. For Jesus' sake. Amen.

God's wise ways

FOR READING AND MEDITATION
PHILIPPIANS 2:1–11

'Each of you should look not only to your own interests, but also to the interests of others.' (v.4)

People, by observation and experimentation, stumble on the truth that is written both in the Scriptures and the universe, namely that God's way is the right way and the only way. A family relations expert who is not a Christian says, 'You must give up yourself. You must serve others or you cannot get along with others.' Here an unbeliever is recognising that self-centredness is not the way – a spiritual issue. Self-focus and self-concern is not the way. If you think of yourself you will become self-conscious; if you think of others you will become other-conscious. The Way is written into our constitutions. We function better physically when we are more concerned about others than we are about ourselves.

O God, when You fashioned me, You fashioned me for Your will and purposes. In them I live – radiantly, rhythmically, abundantly. Amen.

The natural way to live

FOR READING AND MEDITATION
PSALM 119:97–112

'I gain understanding from your precepts; therefore I hate every wrong path.' (v.104)

L ong ago I came to the conclusion that God's way is the natural way to live, and the years, as they have come and gone, have served to reinforce that opinion. Whichever way you approach life – from the Christian revelation, or from science through the facts – you arrive at the same conclusion: life works in God's way. To be good is good for you – for your mind, your soul and your body. To be bad is bad for you – spirit, soul and body. One Christian writer says, 'You must love others or you will not be able to love yourself. Apparently God has us hooked. Anyone who acts differently is a damned fool. And I am not swearing when I say it.'

Father God, I see more clearly than ever that when I am in You, and in Your purposes, I am in the way intended for me. Amen.

Living with mystery

FOR READING AND MEDITATION
JOB 11:1–20

'Can you fathom the mysteries of God? Can you probe the limits of the Almighty?' (v.7)

Now we start to think about my fourth life conviction: that there is a great deal of mystery in life, and simply accepting this is better than striving to find explanations. Without losing the spirit of an explorer, I have become comfortable about living with the fact that some things in life are a complete mystery and will never – here on earth at least – be revealed, I do not wish to give the impression that embracing this fact is easy. It requires an attitude of great humility – the quiet bending of the spirit before the mysteries of the universe and the willingness to recognise that God will not always condescend to give us the illumination for which we plead. Humility equips us to know, and equips us also to be willing not to know.

Loving God and heavenly Father, give me the humility to sit before those mysteries that You do not want to reveal and still worship and enjoy You. Amen.

Being put in place

FOR READING AND MEDITATION
PSALM 4:1–8

'… search your hearts and be silent.' (v.4)

'**M**ystery,' says Dr Larry Crabb, 'has a way of putting us in our place. We are created beings who, in the presence of God, must throw away our test tubes and logical theorems. Like an architect sitting on the rim of the Grand Canyon we can only look in silence.' Mystery silences us. And who likes to be silenced? Pilate became extremely unnerved when Jesus, after His arrest in Gethsemane, refused to answer his questions (Mark 15:3–5). Likewise, when God allows us to be engulfed in mystery and, despite our pleading, does nothing to clarify His purposes, we too tend to panic. If we want to grow in God, then we must throw ourselves more fully upon Him and learn what it means to really trust.

Loving heavenly Father, Your silences are my salvation, Your mystery the motivation for me to trust more deeply. Amen.

Double-mindedness

FOR READING AND MEDITATION
PSALM 39:1–13

'Look away from me, that I may rejoice again ...' (v.13)

We can respond to mystery in one of two ways: we can participate, observe and marvel at the ways of God, or we can allow ourselves to become frustrated. Mystery reveals our double-mindedness. One moment David is venting his frustration on God, another moment he is pleading with Him to listen but then refusing to speak to Him, and finally, in the last verse, asking God to avert His gaze. As I read this psalm I wonder whether David's double-mindedness would have been so obvious if he had not been caught up in the presence of mystery. We might never see how double-minded and inconsistent we are if God did not sometimes allow us to be wrapped in mystery and realise our need of Him.

Father, I realise that sometimes it takes mystery to make my double-mindedness and inconsistencies apparent and reveal my need of You. Amen.

Asking hard questions

FOR READING AND MEDITATION
JOB 23:1–17

'If only I knew where to find him ... I would state my case before him ...' (vv.3–4)

Not only does mystery silence us and expose our double-mindedness, it can also compel us to struggle. In the atmosphere of mystery we are forced to wrestle honestly with God. Mystery draws out of our soul both our desire for God and our demand for explanations or relief. There are some who feel it is impertinent to ask honest questions of God – and so they bury them in the subconscious. But if we draw back from telling God exactly how we feel in the presence of mystery, and refuse to acknowledge our spiritual struggle, we may lose the voice to cry out for mercy. When God questioned Job, Job came to realise that though he was big enough to ask questions, he was not big enough to understand the answers.

Father, I am so grateful that You do not chastise me for my struggling but use it to bring me closer to You. Amen.

'Wake up, God!'

FOR READING AND MEDITATION
PSALM 44:1–26

'Awake, O Lord! Why do you sleep? Rouse yourself!' (v.23)

M ystery disrupts our souls and stirs our emotions in
such a way that it brings to the surface things that
might otherwise not have emerged. Mystery compels us
to ask ourselves hard questions concerning how we really
feel about God. And, if we respond correctly, the result
will be that we enter into a deeper relationship with Him.
Expressing feelings of hurt to God can either take the
form of an unholy diatribe that revels in engaging Him in
a fight, or a passionate and earnest cry that reveals the
depths of our desperation. The expression of that feeling
leaves the psalmist more desperate and hungry for God
than ever. God is sometimes mysterious, but always
remember that His heart and purposes are good.

*O God, may I really learn this lesson: that though I cannot
always understand what You are doing, Your purposes for
me are always good. Amen.*

An inside matter

FOR READING AND MEDITATION
HEBREWS 4:1–16

'… the word of God … judges the thoughts and attitudes of the heart.' (v.12)

My fifth conviction is this: deep spiritual change comes not so much from the outside in, but from the inside out. Change, real change, is an 'inside matter'. It begins at the core of the personality and works its way out. Some of the saddest people in the Church are those who appear all right on the outside, but inside their lives are in a mess. And there are far more of these in the Christian community than we might imagine. Perhaps you are one. Are you trying hard to observe the Bible's teaching and yet still feeling frustrated? Do you read about green pastures and quiet waters but fail to find them? Then follow me carefully over the next few days. Help may be closer than you think.

O Father, Your promise is that You will bring peace and joy to my soul. Change me from the inside out. In Christ's name. Amen.

'Whitewashed tombs'

FOR READING AND MEDITATION
MATTHEW 23:23–39

'You are like whitewashed tombs ... beautiful on the outside but on the inside ... full of ... everything unclean.' (v.27)

One counsellor known to me has this as his simple remedy for all spiritual ills: whatever is right, do more of it. If you went to him for counselling regarding a spiritual problem his advice would be to read more of the Bible, give more time to prayer, and check that you are living in obedience to all of God's principles. Prayer and reading the Scriptures are important – please don't hear me minimising these activities. All of these are good things to do, but usually there is much more in the soul that needs addressing. Our Lord, in today's passage, reserved His harshest criticism for those who gave an outward show of doing all the right things but inside were unchanged.

Gracious and loving heavenly Father, deliver me, I pray, from mere outward conformity. Please transform me on the inside. Amen.

'Doing' is not enough

FOR READING AND MEDITATION
LUKE 11:37–54

'Woe to you, because you are like unmarked graves, which men walk over without knowing it.' (v.44)

I am not saying that obedience to God's principles, as laid down in Scripture, is unimportant. Obedience is required of us at all times. What I am trying to spell out is this: often it is easier to concentrate on doing the correct things – giving the right performance – than facing the troubling things that may be going on inside us. Jumping through spiritual hoops can sometimes be more appealing than pausing to reflect on what may be going on in our soul. People *need* to be insulted if they think that outward conformity is enough. There are far too many people in our churches who, in their behaviour, 'play to the gallery'. The cup looks clean on the outside, but inside it is deeply stained.

Gracious God, help me not to regard it as an insult when You draw my attention to the fact that doing the right things is not enough. Amen.

Wells of our own making

FOR READING AND MEDITATION
JEREMIAH 2:4–13

'My people have … forsaken me, the spring of living water, and have dug their own cisterns …' (v.13)

Here God cuts to the very root of the human condition, and says that problems between Him and His people arise because they prefer to drink from wells of their own making rather than draw in absolute and utter dependence on Him. Why would someone prefer to walk past a fountain of fresh, clean water at which they can drink freely, and dig a well of their own? It doesn't make sense. But then our stubborn, sinful tendencies never do make sense. Our carnal nature so deeply committed to independence, abhors feeling helpless. Yet it is precisely this – the feeling of helplessness – which we must be willing to embrace if we are to become dependent on God and drink from His wells rather than those of our own making.

Change my focus from outward conformity, dear Father, and from doing to trusting. In Jesus' name. Amen.

Drinking first

FOR READING AND MEDITATION
JOHN 7:25–44

'If anyone is thirsty, let him come to me and drink.' (v.37)

God has made us with a great thirst for Him, and only He can quench that thirst. But because our carnal nature abhors the feelings of helplessness we experience when we recognise our dependence on another, we tend to pay lip service to the truth while actually trusting more in ourselves than in Him. This misplaced dependence is at the core of most of our problems, and putting things right on the outside will never resolve the issue. In reality there is only one way. What is required is a radical repentance that involves admitting we are powerless to make our lives work and making the commitment never to move away from the position of dependence on God Himself.

I am a thirsty being, and my thirst needs to be quenched in You and by You. Help me to drink, dear Father, and not just to do. Amen.

A disciplined spirit

FOR READING AND MEDITATION
GALATIANS 5:1–15

'... do not use your freedom to indulge the sinful nature ...'
(v.13)

My sixth life conviction is this: there will be little or no advance in the Christian life without a disciplined spirit. Many who have received the free grace of God then let it leak out because of a lack of discipline. Early on in my ministry I wrongly emphasised freedom to the exclusion of responsibility. A certain woman was, after prayer, healed of paralysis in her legs. However when she asked for prayer about her weight problem the answer came from Matthew 17:21: '... this kind does not go out except by prayer and fasting.' When dependence was necessary for healing, that was the answer. When discipline was necessary, that was the answer. Discipline plus dependence makes dependable disciples.

Lord Jesus Christ, You were so disciplined when You were here on earth – yet so free. Teach me Your secret. Amen.

Love that 'springs'

FOR READING AND MEDITATION
1 TIMOTHY 1:1–11

'... love ... comes from a pure heart and a good conscience and a sincere faith.' (v.5)

Many Christians are afraid of the word 'discipline' as it conjures up an image of a harsh and rigid type of person. But it need not be so. I like the way James Moffatt translates today's text: 'The aim of the Christian discipline is the love that springs from a pure heart, from a good conscience, and from a sincere faith.' Put that way, it shows that the end of discipline is spontaneity – 'love that springs'. Love can spring – that is, be spontaneous and free – only if it comes from a pure heart, a good conscience and a sincere faith. In other words, from a disciplined spirit. Liberty comes through obedience to God's law. No matter what anyone says to the contrary, there is no liberty without discipline.

My Father and my God, help me, I pray, to have a disciplined spirit. Again I surrender myself to the task of making Your disciplines my disciplines. Amen.

My time – His time

FOR READING AND MEDITATION
EPHESIANS 5:15–18

'Be very careful, then, how you live … making the most of every opportunity …' (vv.15–16)

One of the first things that needs to be disciplined is the way we spend our time. This was brought home to me when I read *The Screwtape Letters* by C.S. Lewis. At one point Screwtape advises Wormwood to make sure that a man who has become a Christian 'regards his time as *his* time'. It dawned upon me as I read those words that I had never submitted my time to God because it belongs to Him. I thought that my time was *my* time. Since then I have had a great sense of the stewardship of time. But how do we discipline ourselves to manage time well? We must see that it is not time that needs to be managed so much as ourselves. Often we do what we like doing rather than what we ought to be doing.

O Jesus, as I look at the Gospels I see that You were never in a hurry. Yet You had time for everything God wanted You to do. Amen.

Three life hindrances

FOR READING AND MEDITATION
MATTHEW 18:1–9

'If your hand or your foot causes you to sin, cut it off …'
(v.8)

We must learn not only to discipline our time but to discipline our whole approach to life. In the passage we have read today Jesus speaks metaphorically of three possible life hindrances: the hand, the foot and the eye. The hand is the part of you that takes hold of what you want. It grasps. Be careful, therefore, what you grasp. The foot is what you use to approach the thing desired. Don't walk towards something unless you are willing to take hold of that thing and have it take hold of you. Don't toy with your feelings. The eye looks at the thing you approach and the heart covets. You first see then seek. Discipline the beginnings and the ends will take care of themselves.

Father, I understand that the conclusions in life are dictated by their beginnings. Help me discipline my beginnings. In Jesus' name. Amen.

Seeing things through

FOR READING AND MEDITATION
DEUTERONOMY 5:32–33

'… do what the LORD your God has commanded you;
do not turn aside …' (v.32)

Another aspect of being disciplined is this: make sure you stay with the things you are certain God has called you to do. Be careful that you throw yourself only into those things that God wants you to be involved in. Don't take up everything that comes along. I was struck by this verse in Deuteronomy: 'Be careful not to sacrifice your burnt offerings anywhere you please. Offer them only at the place the LORD will choose …' (Deut. 12:13–14). We must save ourselves to sacrifice our life offering on the altar of the worthwhile. Get guidance from God, know your call and continue in it. That doesn't mean you won't get sidetracked and have to retrace your steps. But discipline yourself to stay with that which is vital.

O God, once more I ask that You will help me become a disciplined person. Please show me what I should, and should not, be doing. Amen.

Celestial bouncers

FOR READING AND MEDITATION
GENESIS 3:14–24

*'After he drove the man out, he placed ... cherubim ...
to guard the way to the tree of life.' (v.24)*

The seventh life conviction I hold is this: life on this planet is exceedingly painful and difficult. At first this might seem rather a pessimistic outlook to take on life, but I have discovered that only when we have faced this fact can we transcend it. When Adam and Eve were banished from the garden they were banished *forever*. God stationed cherubim – celestial bouncers – and a flaming sword to prevent them from returning. They could not go back, they could only go forward. And the way forward was difficult and painful – accompanied by thorns, weeds and frustrating situations. We really cannot go back to Eden. We must go forward through a world that has been upset and tainted by sin – but with Christ's help.

Father please enable me to come to terms with the truth that life in a fallen world can be tough. But You are with me. By Your grace I will win through. Amen.

Taste now – banquet later

FOR READING AND MEDITATION
2 CORINTHIANS 5:1–10

'... God ... has given us the Spirit as a deposit, guaranteeing what is to come.' (v.5)

If we can't go back to Eden what about the possibility of bringing heaven to us? Well, it is possible to have a little bit of heaven to go to heaven in, *but we can't have heaven now*. We can experience a taste of heaven but the full banquet comes later. There are some Christians who believe we *can* have heaven now. The purpose in the minds of those who propagate this kind of teaching (though they may be largely unconscious of it) is to blunt the painful reality of what it's like to live as part of an imperfect, and sometimes evil, society. Thus they learn to pretend that they feel now what they cannot, and will not, feel until they get to heaven. This, I am afraid, is illusion rather than reality.

Father, deliver me, I pray, from all unreality, and help me see that I can depend on You to be with me in every situation. Amen.

A trigger for frustration

FOR READING AND MEDITATION
JOB 5:1–16

'Yet man is born to trouble as surely as sparks fly upward.' (v.7)

When emphasising the theme that life is painful and difficult I have been accused of being a pessimist. I reply that it is better to be a sane pessimist than a silly optimist. Only when we face reality can we overcome it. Oswald Chambers said: 'There will be little progress in the Christian life until we see that life is more tragic than orderly.' Chambers is not denying that good things do happen. Nor is he saying that God does not work through these situations to glorify His name. But tragic events do happen and not to accept and understand this is to live with a false view of life. People with this condition live very frustrated lives and focus more on the way things *should* be than on the way they are.

Father, help me understand the difference between what can be changed and what cannot. And please give me grace to accept the inevitable. Amen.

'Second childhood'

FOR READING AND MEDITATION
HEBREWS 2:5–18

'Because he himself suffered when he was tempted, he is able to help those who are being tempted.' (v.18)

One psychiatrist claims that senility is not just a biological disorder; it can also be a manifestation of a refusal to grow up or to keep on growing. Those who stop growing or learning in their early adulthood, he says, become fixed in their thinking and often lapse into what is called 'second childhood'. They become self-centred and, as Christians, demand that God gives them heaven now. But we can't have heaven at the present time. Then what do we have now? The unimpeachable promise that the Lord will never leave us or forsake us (Heb. 13:5), and that no matter how difficult or even tragic our circumstances, He will stay with us all the way. Our Lord has suffered here on this earth too. He knows what it is to live outside the garden.

Father God, may I walk through this world as Jesus walked – facing all reality, yet conscious of ever present divine strength and power. Amen.

Escapism – the wrong road

FOR READING AND MEDITATION
ROMANS 8:18–27

'... *our present sufferings are not worth comparing with the glory that will be revealed in us.*' (v.18)

We need to beware what is called 'escapism' from the reality of life by having false illusions. Instead we are to face difficulties in the power of the Holy Spirit, move towards others with love, and prove the goodness of God in the midst of our problems. We must remind ourselves, also, that 'our present sufferings are not worth comparing with the glory that will be revealed in us'. This means we must keep our eyes fixed on what lies ahead of us and not allow ourselves to become wedded to this world. Though we are not yet home, the thought of home, as millions of suffering Christians down the ages have testified, can spur us on and motivate us even when we are in the midst of huge problems.

O Lord, help me see that though I am not yet home, the thought of home spurs me forward when I feel like giving up. Amen.

God in His own community

FOR READING AND MEDITATION
GENESIS 1:20–31

'Then God said, "Let us make man in our image, in our likeness ..."' (v.26)

My eighth life conviction is: the most important issue in the universe is that of relationships. Fundamentally God is a relational Being. God is a community – a community of three Persons who relate to one another in perfect harmony. Broughton Knox said: 'We learn from the Trinity that relationship is the essence of reality ... and therefore the essence of our existence.' I had always believed that the ultimate reality was truth but I came to see that it is not the *ultimate* reality. Truth is propositional; relationship is personal. When you touch the heart of the universe you touch not simply an idea, a law or even a thought. You touch a God who *relates*. There is warmth, not just wonder, at the heart of the Trinity.

Father, enable me to realise that the fact You are a relational God is not simply a matter for theologians to discuss – its implications reach every area of my life. Amen.

Nothing more important

FOR READING AND MEDITATION
HEBREWS 8:1–13

'I will be their God, and they will be my people.' (v.10)

In some religions God is presented as a single figure playing 'Solitaire' – a God who needs nobody, feels nothing, but just sits and thinks. In others there is a vast hierarchy of independent gods either fighting one another or doing their own thing. The biblical view of the Trinity cuts right across these false ideas. It presents the truth of one God in three Persons – Father, Son and Holy Spirit – who exist in mutual love and understanding. This relational quality which we see in the Trinity – and this is my main point – is expected also of the people God has created. In other words, loving relationships – love of God and love of others – is what life is all about. Nothing is more important.

Father, help us see that our greatest calling is the quality of our relationships – to be a people who love. In Jesus' name. Amen.

Other-centredness

FOR READING AND MEDITATION
JOHN 13:18–38

'… Love one another. As I have loved you, so you must love one another.' (v.34)

'We learn from the Trinity that the way relationship should be expressed is by concern for others' (Broughton Knox). The energy and power that pulses in the heart of the Trinity is other-centred. By that I mean it is turned outward, not inward. Cynddylan Jones said, 'The best way in which we, the people of God, can reflect the nature of God here on earth is in the way we relate.' But what does it mean to relate well? A good relationship exists when we are using our resources for the wellbeing of others. However, something has gone wrong. Most of us have to admit that we are far more concerned about ourselves than we are about others. Instead of being self-centred we should be more other-centred.

Gracious and loving God, You who relate in glorious other-centredness, help me to do the same. In Jesus' name I pray. Amen.

'Another gospel'

FOR READING AND MEDITATION
1 JOHN 4:13–21

'We love because he first loved us.' (v.19)

God has a very simple pattern for our relationships. First we relate to Him, then to others, and we ourselves come last. However, I am afraid that 'another gospel' is gaining acceptance in the Church at this present time which changes that order around. Attention is focused on loving ourselves so that then, it is said, we are better able to love God and love others. But the biblical model is that first we relate to God by asking Him to forgive our sins and this creates within us a love for Him. Our love for God is then the response to His love for us. Having been filled with God's love, we are then to give ourselves to others. Note the order – freely we have received, freely we give.

O Father, forgive me if I reverse the divine order for relationships by putting myself ahead of others – and perhaps even You. Amen.

The best Xray

FOR READING AND MEDITATION
COLOSSIANS 3:1–17

'... *clothe yourselves with compassion, kindness, humility, gentleness and patience.' (v.12)*

Have you ever wondered why there are so many accounts of relationships in the Bible? It is full of stories of people relating well or not relating well. Almost every problem we have in life will stem from a difficulty in relationships – our relationship with God, with others or with ourselves. Our relationships probably give the best X-ray of the condition of our soul, for our true dedication to God will show itself in the way we relate to Him, to others and to ourselves. Remember, we are not mechanical beings – we are personal, made in God's image. That means there is always something going on between ourselves and others. And what goes on ought, if we are truly His, to reflect His attitude towards us.

O Father, help me to answer the question: Do I reach out to others in the same way that You reach out to me? Amen.

Love – the strongest force

FOR READING AND MEDITATION
I CORINTHIANS 13:1–13

'Love never fails.' (v.8)

M y ninth life conviction is this: love is indeed the strongest force in the universe and will ultimately prevail even over hate. Of course it must be admitted that within the limits of an individual life, and *as far as our own observation goes*, love does sometimes appear to fail. But our vision is temporal and we cannot always see the end of a matter. Hate, however, *never* succeeds, except in producing hate. Blood feuds prove that. Revenge, once it is planted, never needs replanting; it seeds itself. Only loving forgiveness can destroy the terrible weed. It is impossible to stamp out enmity by hate. When the conqueror's foot is on the victim's neck the heart may still be unsubdued.

O God, blow with the breath of Your Spirit on the embers of my heart and set me aflame with love – Your love. In Jesus' name I ask it. Amen.

The taste of love

FOR READING AND MEDITATION
GALATIANS 5:16–26

'But the fruit of the Spirit is love ...' (v.22)

The first fruit of the Spirit is love. Now suppose that any fruit other than love had been put first. Love would then have been second best. Love is first in the list because it belongs there. There is no other place for it but the first place. This agrees with what Paul says in Romans 5:5: '... God has poured out his love into our hearts by the Holy Spirit, whom he has given us.' Some would say that power is the first thing to be sought in the Christian life. Power is important, but love is more important. With good reason the apostle Paul lists the first fruit of the Spirit as love because every other fruit has the taste of love in it.

O God my Father, I see that I need love above everything else. And I need Your unique brand of love. Pour it in, dear Lord. Amen.

Love unlimited

FOR READING AND MEDITATION
ACTS 7:51–60

'Lord, do not hold this sin against them.' (v.60)

The greatest victories in life are secured through love. Stephen, the first Christian martyr, demonstrated the kind of love towards his enemies that our Lord exhibited as He was crucified. The execution of Stephen was something that must have created a great stir. People in Jerusalem had seen Jesus show love to His enemies as they nailed Him to the cross, but now here was one of the Saviour's disciples showing the same love, and using almost the same words that Jesus had used as He was subjected to His grim ordeal at Golgotha. That love conquers hate was demonstrated not only by the Saviour but also by His followers. Here was love unlimited, extending from the heart of the Saviour to His followers.

Father, may I really get hold of the truth that there is no defeat for those who love. Help me to live in victory – the victory of love. Amen.

Heads we win!

FOR READING AND MEDITATION
MATTHEW 10:1–16

'Freely you have received, freely give.' (v.8)

Jesus told His disciples to offer peace to a house.
If the people of the house received it, well and good. If
they did not receive it then the disciples were exhorted
to let the peace return to them. They themselves were
more peaceful for having given the peace – so in either
case they won. It is the same also with us. If we give
love and people receive it, then good. If they don't take
it, it is still good. Heads we win, tails we also win. The
loving person always wins, for he or she becomes more
loving in giving out love, even if the other person doesn't
accept it. 'Love never fails.' It never fails to enrich the
giver, for the more love he or she gives, the more love
they can receive, to give again.

*Father, I accept that to love is always the right thing to do.
Please empower me so that my love will grow stronger and
stronger. Amen.*

Unlove cannot succeed

FOR READING AND MEDITATION
1 CORINTHIANS 16:5–18

'Do everything in love.' (v.14)

Love cannot fail. It is true also to say that the unloving act cannot succeed. If we appear to succeed in accomplishing things by an unloving attitude the success is not real since the unloving attitude or deed – like a loving attitude or deed – registers itself within us. Our whole being is demeaned by unloving behaviour. If love never fails then unlove never succeeds. It cannot by its very nature. This is why we must bestow love, for we are made by the very qualities we exhibit. But is this a practicable way to live? Won't people take advantage of us? Our calling as Christians is to do what is right and leave the consequences to God.

O Father, I see that the closer I get to Jesus, the better I will love. Help me to do everything through love, for love, and by love. Amen.

'A specialist in grace'

FOR READING AND MEDITATION
LUKE 21:1–19

'This will result in your being witnesses to them.' (v.13)

The tenth of my life convictions is: everything that happens to us – good, bad or indifferent – contributes to life if we know how to use it. Moffatt translates today's verse, 'That will turn out an opportunity for you to bear witness.' Everything is an opportunity for those who follow Christ. As God's children we have a 'but' to pit against every circumstance. Paul said, 'I am ... chained ... *But* God's word is not chained' (2 Tim. 2:9). Take, too, Paul's 'thorn in the flesh' (2 Cor. 12:7). We can't be sure what it was, but we know it threw him back upon God's grace to a greater extent than ever before. People saw not a thorn in the flesh but grace. His infirmity furthered him. He became a specialist in grace.

Father, if trouble comes into my life and, after prayer, still remains, help me see that with the resources of Your grace no infirmity can make me infirm. Amen.

A life text

FOR READING AND MEDITATION
ROMANS 8:28–39

'And we know that in all things God works for the good of those who love him ...' (v.28)

I sometimes describe this text as my 'life text'. Some of the events which affect us may, in themselves, be evil, but God works in and through those events to turn them to good. If human beings can transform things such as rubbish tips to beautiful landscaped gardens, what of God? Think again of the cross – that is the supreme example. God took the foulest event that ever happened on this earth and made it into the most sublime. If He can do that with the cross then what can He do with the difficulties and problems that crowd into your life? Even though the things we experience may not be good, and may not of themselves work together for good, 'in all things God works for the good of those who love him'.

O God, You turned the worst thing that happened to Your Son – His death on the cross – into the best thing that could happen for us – our redemption. Thank You that You are working similarly in my life. Amen.

First step

FOR READING AND MEDITATION
JAMES 1:1–15

'Consider it pure joy, my brothers, whenever you face trials of many kinds …' (v.2)

How do we take whatever comes and make it further us? There are three simple steps. Let's consider them one by one. First, we must accept that bad things can happen to us even though we are God's people. That is a fact which we must acknowledge. It's no good fretting and fuming, believing that God should not allow bad things to happen to His own children. Whatever the reason (and we shall not fully fathom this on earth), He does. So try to come to terms with this issue in your heart. And accept it willingly, not grudgingly. God cannot fully work out His purposes in a heart that carries a grudge – whether that grudge be against Him or against others.

My Father and my God, may I not obstruct Your purposes by holding a grudge or by harbouring bitterness in my heart. Help me to accept whatever You permit. Amen.

Learning from everything

FOR READING AND MEDITATION
PROVERBS 1:1–9

'... let the wise listen and add to their learning, and let the discerning get guidance ...' (v.5)

The second step is this: be ready to learn whatever you might need to learn from the experience or situation. For instance, if criticism shatters then ask yourself: Is the criticism true? If so, then correct whatever has been criticised. Make your critics the 'unpaid watchmen of your soul'. If the criticisms are false then look into your heart to see what kind of attitude you are adopting to your critics. Is it one of anger and resentment? If it is, is this telling you something about your spiritual condition? Confess it to God and deal with it. Trouble has a way of highlighting our attitudes, and if the trouble reveals unspiritual ones then thank God for the opportunity to put matters right.

O God, this secret of using everything to further me is so important. I understand the principle. Help me, dear Lord, to apply it. In Jesus' name. Amen.

Believe!

FOR READING AND MEDITATION
MATTHEW 13:47–58

'And he did not do many miracles there because of their lack of faith.' (v.58)

The third step is this: believe in God's ability to turn bad into good. Unbelief can hamper even the Almighty. Today's text tells us that in His home town of Nazareth our Lord was hindered from working miracles because of unbelief. Have you faith, in His power to transform situations? We must work with God towards the desired end. God is able to reveal His purposes to a receptive mind and believing heart in a way that He cannot to the unreceptive. Learn whatever is necessary to learn from our troubles, and have faith in God's power to transform everything. When He makes things plain work with Him. Before matters are plain, be expectant. He will glorify His name.

O Father, from this day forward may I have the set of soul that allows all winds to drive me towards Your goals. Amen.

There's more!

FOR READING AND MEDITATION
2 CHRONICLES 7:11–22

'… if my people … will humble themselves and pray …
then will I hear from heaven …' (v.14)

The eleventh conviction I hold is this: God has more to give us, His Church, in terms of the Holy Spirit than we have yet seen in this generation. It is my firm belief that God is waiting and longing not only to shake the Church with a mighty Holy Spirit revival but, through the Church, to shake some of the world's great nations also. Why, then, does He tarry? The difficulties are always on our side, never on His. Throughout the history of the Church, revival has come on the wings of prevailing prayer. I see no scriptural reason for that to change. God has promised to hear His people's prayers – and He will.

Father, may Your greatest purposes be birthed in Your Church's commitment to prayer. In Christ's name. Amen.

Floods!

FOR READING AND MEDITATION
ISAIAH 44:1–8

'For I will pour water on the thirsty land, and streams on the dry ground …' (v.3)

God sends 'streams on the dry ground'. In the Authorised Version the word used is 'floods'. In fact revival is just that – God flooding a community, or locality, or even a nation with an awesome tide of spiritual power. 'Awe' is not a word we hear often in connection with our church services. We hear words such as worship, reverence, respect but seldom do we hear the word awe. But that is the word frequently heard when God visits His Church in revival power. Some popular choruses have the words 'I stand in awe of You', but do we really experience the awe we sing about, or is it just a matter of words? In revival, awe is not simply an expression; it is an experience.

Father, while we are grateful for every shower of blessing that comes our way, our hearts long for the floods. In Jesus' name we ask it. Amen.

Handle carefully

FOR READING AND MEDITATION
PSALM 85:1–13

'Will you not revive us again, that your people may rejoice in you?' (v.6)

We should not use the word 'revival' to describe a Christian event, such as an evangelistic campaign. Evangelism is the expression of the Church; revival is an experience of the Church. Evangelism is the work we do for God; revival is the work God does for us. Though we must not become slaves to words, I think in the interests of clarity we should refrain from applying the word 'revival' to anything that does not fit the true definition and handle it carefully. Revival is big and beautiful, awesome and majestic, revolutionary and powerful, engulfing and overwhelming, staggering and stunning. Let us not call anything a 'revival' that does not fully accord with all those descriptions.

O God my Father, the more I grasp what real revival is, the more my heart burns with a desire to experience it. Grant it, dear Lord. Amen.

Why we need revival

FOR READING AND MEDITATION
REVELATION 3:14–22

'So, because you are lukewarm … I am about to spit you out of my mouth.' (v.16)

Why do we need a spiritual revival? Why can't the Church live in such a way that revival becomes unnecessary? I believe that the major reason for all spiritual decline is the longing for independence and control. Initially, when we enter into a relationship with God, everything is so new and unfamiliar that we lean upon the Lord in great dependence. It is very easy, however, to then settle down and become spiritually lukewarm, just like the Christians in Laodicea. The believers there wanted their passion to be under their own control. They did not know what it meant to be 'lost in wonder, love and praise'. They needed, like so many of us here in the twenty-first century, to be revived.

O God, forgive us for our unimpassioned Christianity. We repent of our lukewarmness and plead with You to revive us again. Amen.

Times of refreshing

FOR READING AND MEDITATION
ACTS 3:11–26

'Repent, then, and turn to God, so that ... times of refreshing may come from the Lord ...' (v.19)

I am not sure that every nation of the world will see a great moving of the Holy Spirit, but I am convinced that many will. Some say that putting before people the idea of praying for, and expecting, a worldwide outpouring of the Spirit causes them to neglect the issues that need to be confronted in the present, such as evangelism and social action. I have some sympathy with this point of view as I have known many who have become so preoccupied with the subject of revival that they have, indeed, overlooked the needs of the present. The theme of revival may be a passion, but it must not become an obsession that excludes everything else. We are also called to witness and good works.

O God, please prepare my heart to accept the thought that You really do want to pour out floods upon the dry ground. Amen.

Who's the focal point?

FOR READING AND MEDITATION
I CORINTHIANS 10:23–33

'So whether you eat or drink or whatever you do, do it all for the glory of God.' (v.31)

M y final life conviction that I would like to share with you here is this: God's glory must be the point of everything we do. Unless that is so all our efforts will be wrong. The bestsellers in our Christian bookshops are those that tell us how to make our lives more satisfying, more enriching. Not that these matters are unimportant, but some are explored in a self-absorbed way that treats our enjoyment of life as more of a priority than anything else. 'Narcissism,' says the theologian Jim Packer, 'seems to be taking over the modern day Church.' We must therefore ask ourselves: Whose concerns and whose glory dictate what I am doing and the way I am living – mine or God's?

Father, in so many aspects of my life I confess that I make myself the focal point – not You. Please forgive me and help me change. Amen.

The right order

FOR READING AND MEDITATION
ISAIAH 6:1–13

'Holy, holy, holy is the Lord Almighty; the whole earth is full of his glory.' (v.3)

What is the theme of the passage before us today? Isaiah's wellbeing or God's glory? Clearly, it is the glory of God. Scripture tells us that we are created for God's glory (Isa. 43:7), we have fallen short of His glory (Rom. 3:23), and, as we saw yesterday, we are to do everything for His glory (1 Cor. 10:31). At our Lord's birth the angels' message was this: 'Glory to God in the highest, and on earth peace to men on whom his favour rests' (Luke 2:14). This is the right order: God's glory first and humanity's wellbeing second. When we tamper with that order we not only demean God but we also demean ourselves. For we are what we are because He is who He is.

Father, I see this is a truth not merely to be looked at but to be lived out. Help me to put Your glory ahead of everything. Amen.

God esteem

FOR READING AND MEDITATION
2 CORINTHIANS 3:7–18

'... we ... are being transformed into his likeness with ever-increasing glory ...' (v.18)

Dr Larry Crabb makes the point that modern Christians have been busy (albeit unconsciously) reducing God to someone useful – a power whose reason for existence is to make our lives more satisfying. In every Christian's heart there is a desire to know God, but all too often it is not so that we might bring Him glory but so that we might gain some benefits for ourselves. This preoccupation with self-esteem has to be resisted, not because self-esteem is unimportant, but because the way to experience it is not through self-effort but through a close encounter with God. What we ought to be focusing on is not self-esteem but God-esteem. The more we hold God in esteem, the more we hold ourselves in esteem.

O God, forgive me for struggling to raise my self-esteem instead of finding it in You. To see myself clearly I must see You clearly. Amen.

Victim or agent?

FOR READING AND MEDITATION
I PETER 4:1–11

'... so that in all things God may be praised through Jesus Christ.' (v.11)

What happens if we do not make the glory of God our primary purpose and goal? When this is the case we tend to put human interests before God's interests. This is something I see happening, for instance, in the field of Christian counselling, where the emphasis is moving from counselling for the glory of God to counselling for the wellbeing of people. Not that people's wellbeing is unimportant. It most certainly is. But there is something more important – *the glory of God*. If those who are involved in counselling do not have this fact in focus then they will be inclined to see the person they are counselling as more of a victim of evil than an agent of God's glory.

O God, forgive me if I regard myself as more of a victim than an agent. Help me bring You glory in all things. Amen.

The bottom line

FOR READING AND MEDITATION
ACTS 10:23–48

*'I now realise how true it is that God does not show
favouritism …' (v.34)*

I am trying to convey the concept of bringing pleasure
to the Almighty by a commitment to put Him first in
everything. We must have a vision of God's character,
particularly His glory. When Peter was persuaded to go
to the Gentiles, and present to them the things God
wanted them to know, he did not say he had discovered
something of the great spiritual needs of the Gentiles
while he was in prayer on the housetop. Rather, he refers
to the fact that he has learned something new about
the character and nature of God. The interests and needs
of people are important, but they must never be the
bottom line. God's glory must be the bottom line. For it
is only as He is glorified that we are glorified.

*O Father, fill me with a vision of Your glory. Whatever has
been my motive before, from now on let me live for Your
glory alone. In Christ's name. Amen.*

'Except for these chains'

FOR READING AND MEDITATION
ACTS 26:19–32

'… I pray God that … you … may become what I am, except for these chains.' (v.29)

This is one of the most amazing moments in Paul's career. He faced death yet his life convictions held, for at the core of his life he was secure. His life convictions had become him. They were one. How sad when the opposite is the case – when people's convictions fall apart. But I have no fear of the convictions I have shared with you in this series falling apart. No longer do I hold them; rather, they hold me. They have become part of my life. They are me. You can't go through life merely with opinions. You must have convictions. And the only convictions that hold are those that are based on God's truth. Nothing else is good enough.

O God, may all my convictions be based on Your truth, and may they deepen so that they are not just something I hold, but something that holds me. Amen.

'Only now and then'

FOR READING AND MEDITATION
GENESIS 6:1–22

'So make yourself an ark of cypress wood; make rooms in it and coat it with pitch ...' (v.14)

The theme for the next two months – Surprised by God – came from the writings of the noted theologian, Frederick Buechner, who said: 'We see God's work clearly *only now and then.*' The point he was making is that God doesn't allow us to see everything clearly all the time, but prefers now and then to break into our lives with delightful and sometimes unsettling surprises. Scripture is filled with accounts of God's surprises whether it is Noah building an ark, Moses at the burning bush or the birth and later resurrection of Jesus. God's surprises in your life and mine may not be quite as dramatic as these, but each one is significant nevertheless.

O Father, help me not to miss Your surprises and, above all, to understand them. In Christ's name I pray. Amen.

Surprises – easy to miss

FOR READING AND MEDITATION
PSALM 103:1–22

'He made known his ways to Moses, his deeds to the people of Israel …' (v.7)

It is easy to go through life missing God's surprises because we don't know how to spot them or, conversely, to 'spiritualise' ordinary events and read into them more than we should. A hunter in Canada once stalked a rare albino deer in a thick forest only to discover that it was, in fact, an abandoned washing machine! Sometimes God's surprises explode in our lives like firecrackers; at other times we squint into the forest, wondering if what we see really is an albino or just an abandoned washing machine. Every one of us needs to understand the reasons why God delights to surprise us. Then we shall be less likely to miss His surprises – or misinterpret them.

Father please make me alert to the ways in which You work in my life so that I shall not miss what You are doing. In Jesus' name I ask it. Amen.

The light that scorches

FOR READING AND MEDITATION
ISAIAH 21:1–17

'My heart falters … the twilight I longed for has become a horror to me.' (v.4)

I saiah asked God for light on the troubling situation of his day. He pleaded for insight and vision that he might see what was hidden from the eyes of others. And God gave him light! His prayer was answered! The darkness yielded to a growing twilight. He saw, but what he saw filled his soul with horror, and caused him almost to wish he did not know what he now knew. The answer we get to our prayers is not necessarily the answer our hearts desire. When we go down on our knees and ask God for illumination, we cannot complain if the light He sends scorches at times with its fierce heat, or be surprised that in response to our request for guidance we are shown things we might have preferred not to have known.

Father, though I may be surprised at the way You sometimes answer my prayers, help me not to react adversely. Amen.

Pain in answered prayer

FOR READING AND MEDITATION
HABAKKUK 1:1–17

'I am raising up the Babylonians, that ruthless and impetuous people ...' (v.6)

Christians talk a good deal about the pain of *unanswered* prayer. But what about the pain of *answered* prayer? What about the light God sends that blisters and burns? How could God use a pagan nation to prune and purify His own people? This revelation, of course, led to Habakkuk becoming aware of a whole new context in which to think about God, and he emerged with a faith that triumphed over everything – even confusion. Keep in mind that when God surprises you by answering your prayers in a way you didn't expect, it is not because He is being irritable. He is giving you a greater opportunity to trust Him, and thus to develop a deeper and richer relationship with Himself.

Father, I see that when I receive answers I did not expect it is so that I can use them as stepping stones to an even deeper trust in You. Amen.

Not the answer we expect

FOR READING AND MEDITATION
LUKE 18:18–30

'You still lack one thing. Sell everything you have …
Then come, follow me.' (v.22)

Today we examine the attitude of the rich young ruler who said to Jesus, 'Good teacher, what must I do to inherit eternal life?' (v.18). Our Lord is not against people having wealth; He is only against them making wealth their god. The first place in any man or woman's life is God's place. The rich young ruler, when he heard our Lord's response, might have said, as did Isaiah, 'The twilight I longed for …' (Isa. 21:4). But the young man, fine though he was in character, loved his wealth more than he loved God. It was the number one thing in his life. That was why Jesus condemned it. We take a risk when we ask God to let us in on His mind and purposes for our lives. Sometimes He tells us things we might prefer not to know.

Father, help me never to let the possibility of being surprised by You hinder me from wanting to discover Your purposes for my life. Amen.

'Simply proclaim the gospel'

FOR READING AND MEDITATION
1 CORINTHIANS 2:1–16

'My message and my preaching were not with wise and persuasive words ...' (v.4)

A minister by the name of Thomas Champness was appointed by his denomination to be the district evangelist to Newcastle upon Tyne, in the north of England. Hearing of the appointment, he rededicated himself to God, and asked the Lord for a word that would help him carry out his task. The word came, but it was not the kind of message he expected. God said this: 'If you are to concentrate exclusively on winning men and women to Me, you must be careless of your reputation as a preacher.' Thomas Champness had already gained a great reputation as a preacher – a reputation of which he was mildly proud. And God said, 'Give it up!' He was to simply proclaim the gospel and proclaim it simply!

O God, help me see that whatever sacrifices I am called to make in Your service, they are as nothing compared to the sacrifice that You made for me. Amen.

Prayer – a risky business

FOR READING AND MEDITATION
ISAIAH 6:1–13

'Woe to me! … For I am a man of unclean lips … and my eyes have seen the King …' (v.5)

When Augustine turned to God and asked for divine illumination on the dark problems of his day, God answered his prayer, but the first thing the light revealed was Augustine's own unchastity and lack of self-control. Augustine talks of how God's light scorched him at times with its intensity and made him aware of things that previously he had preferred not to look at. The Almighty is too eager for our highest good to deny us His healing truth. Sometimes, though, He is unable to get through to us until our hearts are found in the attitude of passionate, persevering prayer. To pray for light and illumination is a risky business, but one that is *always* well worth the risk.

O Father, help me to be prepared for whatever Your light reveals in me. In Christ's name I pray. Amen.

The tilt of the soul

FOR READING AND MEDITATION
JAMES 4:1–17

'Come near to God and he will come near to you.' *(v.8)*

P rayer tilts the soul in the direction of God, and in turn gives God an opportunity to move into the centre of our lives. We bring to God in prayer a personal concern, and He responds by saying, 'Now I have your attention, there's this other matter we could talk about. To you it might not seem as important as your concerns, but it is vital to the wellbeing of your soul.' We shouldn't really be surprised to discover that when we bring personal matters to God in prayer He says, 'You want to talk about *that*, but I want to talk about *this*.' Though we might prefer that He didn't change the subject, believe me, it is always His great love and concern for us that motivates Him to do so.

Father, forgive me for being more concerned that my needs are met than being the person You want me to be. Please help me to get this issue straight. Amen.

No pretending

FOR READING AND MEDITATION
2 CORINTHIANS 3:7–18

'And we ... are being transformed into his likeness with ever-increasing glory ...' (v.18)

We never fully see ourselves until we see ourselves in God. When faced with what He shows us we may be surprised and upset. People respond in different ways to God's surprising answers to their prayers. Some, I have discovered, positively dislike Him for revealing to them more than they bargained for. If we are to avoid going backwards in our Christian lives we need to realise that once we open our hearts to God in prayer then He is likely to expose us to ourselves and help us unlock the chambers of our heart where we are keeping things hidden. We can pretend to others, but God will never let us pretend to Him. In His presence smug complacency vanishes like dew in the scorching heat of the midday sun.

Father, I am comforted to know that You love me too much to shield me from the truth. Help me to press on with You. Amen.

Walk on

FOR READING AND MEDITATION
JOHN 3:16–21

'Everyone who does evil hates the light … for fear that his deeds will be exposed.' (v.20)

We can turn our back when God, through the Holy Spirit, identifies something in our life of which He does not approve, but by turning our back we have not cleansed our heart or restored our soul. It is absurd, of course, to turn away in anger or hostility when God does this, for He only holds the mirror. The impurities are all in us. There is only one thing to do when we tremble in the blinding light of some new revelation: march into the light with God. Pain or no pain – we should march on. The trembling will pass, and we will prove the power of God to strengthen the weak hands and strengthen the feeble knees (see Isa. 35:3).

Father, help me never to be afraid to pray for the light even though it may reveal more than I wish. Help me not to turn back but to walk on. Amen.

'The great surprise'

FOR READING AND MEDITATION
JOHN 3:1–15

'The wind blows wherever it pleases ... So it is with everyone born of the Spirit.' (v.8)

Another way in which we are 'surprised by God' is the manner in which the Holy Spirit brings about the critical experience we call 'conversion'. Oswald Chambers said, 'The element of surprise is always the note of the Holy Ghost in us. We are born again by the great surprise.' Christian conversion cannot happen without the Holy Spirit. Sometimes conversion is spoken of in the Church as if it were the work of men and women. The word conversion is made up of *con*, meaning 'with', and *vertere*, meaning 'to turn'. Conversion is not just turning, but turning *with*. The 'with' introduces us to the Holy Spirit, and the element of the Spirit in conversion makes it a new birth. No Holy Spirit – no conversion.

Father, thank You for turning my life around. May the same Holy Spirit who saved me be ever present in my life to sanctify me. Amen.

As unpredictable as the wind

FOR READING AND MEDITATION
ROMANS 11:5–36

'How unsearchable his judgments, and his paths beyond tracing out!' (v.33)

Jesus pointed out that the Spirit's coming to men and women is as mysterious and unpredictable as the wind. First, *the wind blows where it wills*. That suggests a sovereign element that cannot be controlled. People have learned how to control many things, but they have not yet learned how to control the wind. Harness it – yes. But control it – no. Second, *we hear its sound but cannot see it*. This means it is invisible. The keenest eye is unable to detect it. Third, *we can't tell from where it comes or where it will go*. This means the course of the wind is a mystery. The Holy Spirit works sovereignly, secretly and mysteriously. And He comes to whom He wills, when He wills, and where He wills.

My Father and my God, Your ways are often beyond my comprehension but that doesn't mean I am unable to appreciate them. Amen.

'A man came among us'

FOR READING AND MEDITATION
ROMANS 8:1–17

'You ... are controlled ... by the Spirit, if the Spirit of God lives in you.' (v.9)

Williiam Lecky, the historian, tells of the surprise John Wesley received when he went rather unwillingly to a meeting in London. At about a quarter to nine, John Wesley felt his own heart 'strangely warmed'. He later said: 'An assurance was given me that He had taken away my sins, even mine, and saved me from the law of sin and death.' This strange and unexpected warming of the heart resulted in a moral cleansing of the soul of Britain and the world. Many years after Wesley had died, a visitor to Cornwall commented to a local tin miner, 'You seem to be a very temperate people here. How did it happen?' The miner replied, 'There came a man among us once, and his name was John Wesley.'

O Father, what amazing things You can do through one person who is wholly committed to You. Fill me to overflowing with Your Holy Spirit. Amen.

'Chance' encounter

FOR READING AND MEDITATION
PSALM 92:1–15

'How great are your works, O LORD, how profound your thoughts!' (v.5)

Spiritual conversion is not a matter of chance. The Holy Spirit moves in the most surprising ways to bring about the conversion of a human soul. A certain preacher on his way to conduct a service in a British coastal town stepped into a shop doorway to shelter from a downpour of rain. Another man sheltered there too. Both remarked on the inclemency of the weather and, as the conversation developed, the preacher explained the purpose of his visit. The other man appeared to know next to nothing about Christian churches, but willingly accepted an invitation to attend the service. That night he made the decision to follow Christ. His life was changed because of a 'chance' encounter in a shop doorway.

O Father, what joy fills my soul as I think of the fact that every day Your Spirit is at work drawing people to Yourself. Amen.

Sudden conversions

FOR READING AND MEDITATION
MATTHEW 7:1–24

'By their fruit you will recognise them.' (v.16)

Lacordaire, the French clergyman who once occupied the pulpit of the Cathedral of Notre Dame in Paris, said, 'I was unbelieving in the evening, on the morrow a Christian, certain with an invincible certainty.' Some conversions are gradual, and some are sudden. Some unfold like a flower to the sun – little by little. Others are a sudden leap into the arms of God. Which of these two types of experience is more valid? Both are equally valid. It is not the phenomena associated with conversion that make it valid; what counts, as our text for today tells us, is that 'by their fruit you will recognise them'. After all, the best evidence you are alive is never your birth certificate!

O God, I am so thankful for the experience of my own conversion. May the wonder of it never fade. It began in a miracle and is sustained by a miracle. Amen.

Saved and sobered!

FOR READING AND MEDITATION
ROMANS 1:8–17

'… the gospel … is the power of God for the salvation of everyone who believes …' (v.16)

Dr E. Stanley Jones tells how he once witnessed the conversion of a man who was drunk. Preaching from a soapbox in a public square in Harrodsburg, Kentucky, he asked an inebriated man standing in front of him, 'Do you want to be converted?' 'I'm drunk,' the man responded. 'God can save you drunk or not drunk,' retorted Stanley Jones. 'If you say so it must be so,' conceded the man as he knelt in prayer. Suddenly he opened his eyes, looked around in surprise, and exclaimed, 'Why, He has saved me, and I'm drunk too.' Soon he was completely sober. God saved him and sobered him in minutes. How much more dramatic than that can you get?

My Father and my God, Your grace and might are beyond the power of my mind to measure. All honour and glory be to Your precious name. Amen.

Three-fifths of the way

FOR READING AND MEDITATION
ROMANS 10:1–21

'Everyone who calls on the name of the Lord will be saved.' (v.13)

If you look at Romans 10 you will see that everyone reading these lines is at least three-fifths of the way into the kingdom of God. Five important facts are clearly spelled out. (1) Everyone who calls on the name of the Lord will be saved. (2) No one can call on the One in whom they have not believed. (3) No one can believe in the One of whom they have not heard. (4) No one can hear without someone telling them. (5) No one can tell the story of Christ unless they have been sent. I am sent, I have told you and you have heard. The last two steps are these: believe in the Lord Jesus Christ, then call upon Him.

O God, I take these last two steps in simple faith, believing in Christ to cleanse me of sin and receiving Jesus into my heart as my Lord and my Saviour. Amen.

Glory in the commonplace

FOR READING AND MEDITATION
GENESIS 28:1–22

'How awesome is this place! This is … the house of God …'
(v.17)

Another way in which we find ourselves 'surprised by God' is when He reveals Himself to us at the most unexpected times and in the most unexpected places. The passage we have read today is an illustration of this for who would expect to meet God out there on the barren hillside? Yet that was where God came to Jacob. God's favoured way of meeting His children is, of course, around His Word, the Bible, but this does not mean He will meet us only there. He does not wait for what we might call the 'grand moments' of life. Sometimes He surprises us by making the commonplace grand. And besides, Galilee and Glasgow are just the same to Him.

Father, though Your principal way of revealing Yourself is through the Scriptures, I can meet You also in the ordinary and unexpected places of life. Amen.

'Crammed with heaven'

FOR READING AND MEDITATION
EXODUS 3:1–15

'So Moses thought, "I will go over and see this strange sight …"' (v.3)

I am not arguing that we should abandon the usual paths to knowing God, such as listening to Him when we pray, and eagerly reading the Bible. I am simply saying we should be alert and ready to discover the revelation of God in the common places of life. Elizabeth Barrett Browning penned the famous lines: *Earth's crammed with heaven, And every common bush afire with God.* It is possible to walk about blind to the glory that is around us because we do not expect to find it there. For that reason we need the discerning eye – the power to see the glory in the ordinary, to walk down familiar pathways and notice unfamiliar things, and to hear the accent of Jesus in spite of a dialect.

O God, give me the discerning eye that discovers You in the commonplace and the unexpected. In Jesus' name. Amen.

A muffled cry

FOR READING AND MEDITATION
MATTHEW 25:31–46

'For I was hungry and you gave me something to eat …'
(v.35)

A missionary couple in a Nairobi slum entered a hut and found a woman with an infant in her arms. The woman told them that she was unable to have children, and her prayer, like Hannah in the Old Testament, had been that God would give her a child. One day she heard the muffled cries of an infant. Rushing to a pile of rubbish, she found a tiny baby – cold and abandoned. Had God answered her prayer? First she took the child to the police and then she asked for permission to keep the baby. The authorities agreed. So, clean and warm, the child slept peacefully in this woman's arms. That muffled cry, she believed (and so do I), was the faint reminder that the Spirit of the living Christ is everywhere.

My Father and my God, forgive me if I have overlooked the fact that You can make Yourself known in any place. Amen.

Hush – God is at work!

FOR READING AND MEDITATION
PSALM 139:1–24

'If I go up to the heavens, you are there; if I make my bed in the depths, you are there.' (v.8)

I once overheard a conversation on an airplane. One woman admitted to the other, 'I was very self-centred and lived to enjoy myself until my Down's baby arrived. But she brought such love into the life of my husband and myself that through it we glimpsed the love of God. We both became Christians because of her.' 'A similar thing happened to my husband and me,' said the other woman. 'When our Down's baby was born we drank heavily to drown the sorrow and both became alcoholics. After a while, though, things changed, and the love that flowed from our baby to us was also the means of bringing us to Christ.' I tell you quite frankly that I met God in a new way as I listened in to that conversation.

O Father, sensitise me to the fact that Your Spirit is present to bring glory to Your name in everything and through everything. Amen.

The ordinariness of Jesus

FOR READING AND MEDITATION
JOHN 14:1–14

'Jesus answered: "Don't you know me, Philip, even after I have been among you such a long time?"' (v.9)

Some Christians seem incapable of seeing or finding God in the commonplace. They tend to deny the nobility of anything that mingles with our earthly clay. It does not surprise me that Philip failed to recognise Jesus as God, for human nature is always more attracted to the spectacular than the truly great. If God had come to earth in a chariot of fire, multitudes would have knelt before Him. If He had moved among people with a shining face and dazzling robes, aristocrats would have sought Him out. But He was born as we are born, and so blended the sublime with the normal that only the few saw the sublime was there. I am constantly staggered by the ordinariness of Jesus – aren't you?

Lord Jesus, Your humility and ordinariness overwhelm me. Teach me not to miss the sublime simply because it is clothed in everyday garb. Amen.

Reach out – now

FOR READING AND MEDITATION
JOHN 12:37–50

'When he looks at me, he sees the one who sent me.' (v.45)

G od came to earth in Jesus in a particularly
unspectacular way and, despite the beauty and
perfection of His life, the reason so few recognised Him
was because He mingled the commonplace with the
glorious, and walked along a path trodden by ordinary
men and women. He usually passed unrecognised in
the midst of people. God was *with* humankind and yet
people sought Him afar in magnificent temples. People
seek at a distance the God who stands before them at
the door of their heart. They are waiting for a ladder to
be thrown down from heaven, while all the time Christ
has descended the ladder and is right there beside them.
If you have never received Christ as Saviour, reach out
now. Now!

*O God, forgive me that I have looked for You afar while in
reality You are so near. I reach out to You now. Please save
me. In Jesus' name. Amen.*

'Sweep under the mats'

FOR READING AND MEDITATION
ACTS 10:1–23

'Simon, three men are looking for you. So get up and go downstairs.' (vv.19–20)

There are times when the words God speaks to us seem very ordinary. Looking at today's text, notice how straightforward the message is. The Spirit told him, 'Three men are looking for you. So get up and go downstairs.' The words were simple, direct, and could be spoken by anyone, anywhere, at any time. C.H. Spurgeon was fond of telling the story of his housemaid, who informed him that the day she began to work for him she knelt by her bedside and dedicated herself to keeping house for him. After prayer she asked God for a word, and this is what He said: 'Remember to sweep under the mats.' Yes, it's ordinary – absurdly so. But then God is concerned with ordinary things.

O Father, even ordinary words that come from Your mouth become extraordinary as they are heard in my heart. I am so thankful. Amen.

Shavings of gold

FOR READING AND MEDITATION
ECCLESIASTES 9:1–10

'Whatever your hand finds to do, do it with all your might …' (v.10)

If we are not prepared to meet God in the commonplace we may miss many of His messages to our hearts. I read an old legend of an angel who came one evening to the edge of a river and asked the boatman to ferry him across. The angel rewarded the boatman with a handful of what appeared to be wooden shavings. In disgust the boatman threw them into the river. The next morning he found a few of the shavings still lying in his boat, and examining them more closely found they were shavings of pure gold. Life is filled with so many ordinary moments. Whatever you do, don't treat the ordinary moments as worthless shavings to be thrown away in annoyance because you have received nothing better.

O God my Father, help me be more alert and ready to look for You in the ordinary and the commonplace. Amen.

Not delivered *from*, but delivered *in*

FOR READING AND MEDITATION
ECCLESIASTES 1:1–18

'For with much wisdom comes much sorrow ...' (v.18)

The words 'surprised by God' instinctively bring to mind such wonders as miracles, blessings and last-minute rescues from difficult situations. But God also sends His surprises through pain. As I have mentioned before, 'life is more tragic than orderly' (Oswald Chambers). It's astonishing how many Christians refuse to acknowledge this fact and, like an ostrich, bury their heads in the sand. But denial – the unwillingness to accept reality – gets us nowhere. The surprises of God that we discover in the midst of our difficulties are not always deliverance *from*, but deliverance *in*. But be assured: deliverance *in* is no less a deliverance than deliverance *from*.

O Father, help me understand that though life in a fallen world may be more tragic than orderly, You are at work in everything. You allow only what You can use. Amen.

Voicing questions

FOR READING AND MEDITATION
JEREMIAH 20:7–18

'O Lord, you deceived me, and I was deceived …' (v.7)

To face life realistically we sometimes have to ask difficult questions. I watched the film *Schindler's List* and found myself saying, 'God, how could You have let these things happen? And to the very people who are supposed to be close to You – the Jews?' Was God upset with me because I gave voice to these questions? I do not believe so. He wasn't upset with Jeremiah when he said, 'O Lord, you deceived me', and I don't believe He was upset with me either. God prefers us to bring our hard questions out into the open rather than pretend they are not there. He won't always answer us, but we will find, as Jeremiah found, that He rewards His sincere but confused followers with a richer sense of His presence.

O God, I am thankful that You are not against me for asking hard questions. Amen.

Job's Bar exam

FOR READING AND MEDITATION
JOB 38:1–18

'Brace yourself like a man; I will question you, and you shall answer me.' (v.3)

In today's passage God turns the tables on Job by asking *him* some searching questions. It is as if God is saying, 'Job, you want to plead your case before Me in the courts of justice and ask Me some hard questions. Well, first I have some questions for you: "Where were you when I laid the earth's foundations? ... Who marked off its dimensions? ... Who stretched a measuring line across it?"' (vv.4–5). One after the other the questions came. Job was nonplussed, but eventually he got the point: there were some things he would never understand, and because God is who He is, He should be taken on trust. He didn't have his questions answered but he did see God and have a richer awareness of Him (42:5). That was enough.

Loving heavenly Father, help me reach the place Job arrived at so that when answers do not come I can take You on trust. Please reveal Yourself to me. Amen.

Everything – for the best

FOR READING AND MEDITATION
LAMENTATIONS 3:1–26

'... *great is your faithfulness. I say to myself, "The LORD is my portion ..."' (vv.23–24)*

Early in my ministry I went to console a widow whose husband had died in a mining accident and tried to explain why God had let it happen. She listened for a while but then said, 'I don't need to understand all that. What I do need is a God who is bigger than my understanding, a God who knows so much more than me.' That mild reproach went home, I can assure you. It was one of the greatest lessons of my life. Sometimes I wonder if trying to interpret the ways of God to people becomes counterproductive. Perhaps there is more solace in simply recognising that God is bigger than we are, and that we can trust Him to work out everything for the best.

Gracious Father, please help me trust You to bring all things to a good and perfect end. In Jesus' name. Amen.

Our grief – His grief

FOR READING AND MEDITATION
1 PETER 2:13–25

'… Christ suffered for you, leaving you an example, that you should follow in his steps.' (v.21)

God not only looks down in love when we are caught up in tragedy, not only weeps with us as we are surrounded by the flames, but reaches down into the flames to soothe and support. And His own hands get scorched in the process. Some think God is impervious to the pains that afflict our lives. I tell you He is affected by them – and affected deeply. He hurts in our hurts. Always remember, His own family – the Trinity – have known grief too. And grief of the greatest magnitude. He saw His own Son skewered to a Roman cross. Yes, this great God of the universe knows what it is to experience pain. Our sufferings are His sufferings.

O merciful Father, I see that Your heart too has experienced grief and pain, and indeed all our griefs are Yours. Amen.

Are you willing?

FOR READING AND MEDITATION
MARK 9:14–32

'I do believe; help me overcome my unbelief!' (v.24)

If God is loving, as He says he is, why doesn't He do something about your painful situation? 'Why?' is the easiest question to ask, but not the easiest to answer. It's not wrong to air the question if something is troubling you, but try not to become obsessed about the matter. The best position to take in times of perplexity is the position of trust. Though not easy, adopting the same approach to the Lord as the man in our passage today will produce amazing results in the soul: 'I do believe; help me overcome my unbelief!' The principle is this: when complete trust is difficult, first identify the fact that you already have some trust, then ask for more. You will receive from God only as much as you are *willing* to receive.

O God, please enable me to grasp this principle this very day. I believe … now help me overcome my unbelief. You are ready, I am willing. Amen.

Pain – 'God's megaphone'

FOR READING AND MEDITATION
2 CORINTHIANS 12:1–10

'Three times I pleaded with the Lord to take it [a thorn in my flesh] away from me.' (v.8)

C.S. Lewis said: 'Pain is God's megaphone to rouse a deaf world.' Sometimes this is the only way God can get our attention; pain becomes His 'megaphone'. One has only to read his book *Miracles* to see the confidence Lewis placed in the supernatural power of God. But what do we do when God doesn't heal or respond to our predicament with a demonstration of miraculous power? We look for Him to surprise us in another way – by finding a secret stair to our soul and coming to us in a way that strengthens us and enables us to go through the difficulties with spiritual poise and calm. This is what it means to live by God's surprises. If the surprise doesn't come in one way, it comes in another.

Holy Spirit, I see that You are continually trying to unfold truth to my heart. Help me to hear You sooner. In Christ's name I pray. Amen.

Our 'terrible freedom'

FOR READING AND MEDITATION
JOHN 10:1–10

'... I have come that they may have life, and have it to the full.' (v.10)

We look now at the surprise that most people experience following their conversion when they discover that, in addition to having their sins forgiven, their hearts are filled with a deep and lasting joy. Before my conversion I had never associated Christianity with joy but with rigorous duty and discipline and about as appealing to me as going to prison. Why are we so surprised when, having surrendered to Him, we find His words to be true? One reason, I think, is because to hold on to the concept of God as a killjoy makes it easier to justify our unwillingness to surrender to His claims. Of course, refusing to surrender is our freedom but, as C.S. Lewis put it, it is 'a terrible freedom'.

Father, how thankful I am that of all the surprises that came to me following my conversion, one of the greatest was the discovery of joy. Amen.

'Glorious joy'

FOR READING AND MEDITATION
I PETER 1:1–12

'… you believe in him and are filled with an inexpressible and glorious joy …' (v.8)

In *Surprised By Joy* C.S. Lewis wrote of his conversion – that he was 'invaded' by joy. Christian joy is, of course, different from happiness. Happiness is dependent on circumstances. If what happens happens happily then we are happy. But joy is different. Joy is that deep and enduring sense that all is well, even when circumstances are against us. A Roman Catholic woman who experienced a sound spiritual conversion said in amazement, 'Strange, but I never associated joy with God before.' Now, despite almost impossible domestic difficulties, she describes herself as 'abounding with joy'. She is joyful *in spite of*! That is real joy. If, when we come to Christ, we are surprised by joy, the surprise ought to be that we are surprised.

O Father You are so gracious, so forgiving and so understanding. My joy and gratitude know no bounds. Amen.

'Tell your face about it'

FOR READING AND MEDITATION
PSALM 105:1–11

'… let the hearts of those who seek the LORD rejoice.' (v.3)

S ome Christians have given the impression that the Christian life is anything but full and joyful. Far too often our general attitude suggests that Christianity is a heavy load which we are carrying rather than a living faith which carries us. One day a Christian, who was a somewhat grim-looking individual, paused while a Salvation Army open-air meeting was being held in the East End of London. A young Salvation Army girl, hovering on the outskirts of the crowd, approached him and asked him if he was saved. Embarrassed by the question, he replied tartly, 'Of course I am.' 'Well, sir,' she advised, 'I suggest that as soon as possible you tell your face about it!' Challenging words, but they went home.

O God, Help us open our hearts to more of Your joy so that our faces glow with Your eternal joy. In Jesus' name. Amen.

Not good examples?

FOR READING AND MEDITATION
MATTHEW 5:13–20

'... let your light shine before men, that they may see your good deeds and praise your Father ...' (v.16)

Uncomfortable though it may be to consider, we Christians have to face the fact that many of us are not always good examples of the faith we profess. We may not swear, steal, get drunk or commit acts of violence, but neither do thousands of other people who make no claim to be Christians. It's a terribly challenging question I am about to ask you but I have asked it of myself also: What does our Christianity do for us? By our attitudes are we nullifying the Christian message? Does our behaviour contradict the very truths we are trying to get across to others? If Christians are, by definition, people in whom Christ lives, then should we not be showing more evidence that the risen Christ is alive in us?

My Father and my God, I have found in You the ultimate joy. May I not only be alive in You but look alive also. In Jesus' name I pray. Amen.

All will be well

FOR READING AND MEDITATION
2 CORINTHIANS 4:1–18

'... *persecuted, but not abandoned; struck down, but not destroyed.*' (v.9)

Does what I am saying mean that Christians have to go about wearing a fixed smile even when they are about to attend the funeral of a person they loved dearly? No, God does not expect that, and neither does the world. It is perfectly legitimate to show sorrow, to cry, and to feel hurt when life is painful and full of trouble. Our faith as Christians does not insulate us from feelings of hurt, grief and sorrow. What, then, does it mean to have and to express Christian joy? It means that regardless of what is happening, there is an underlying sense that in the final analysis *all will be well*. Joy didn't keep the apostle Paul from being knocked down, but it did keep him from being knocked out.

Father, I see that the joy You provide is not the kind that eliminates sorrow, but transforms it into something else so all will be well. Amen.

'Your halo is too tight'

FOR READING AND MEDITATION
HEBREWS 12:1–13

'... Jesus ... for the joy set before him endured the cross ...'
(v.2)

Have you noticed how many comedians include not only jokes about mothers-in-law but miserable Christians as well? Once I heard one say, 'A born-again Christian went to his doctor and complained, "I've got a persistent headache that will not go away." "Do you smoke?" asked the doctor. "No." "Drink?" "No." "Go dancing?" "No." "Sleep around?" "No." The doctor thought for a moment and said, "I think I know what's wrong with you. Your halo is too tight."' Certainly there are some miserable Christians, but they didn't get their misery from their Christian faith. Most likely it was there before they became Christians, and they have never allowed the joy that Christ gives to break through.

O Father, help us not only to lay hold on joy but to let it lay hold on us also. In Christ's name. Amen.

Our birthright

FOR READING AND MEDITATION
LUKE 15:1–10

'… there is rejoicing in the presence of the angels of God over one sinner who repents.' (v.10)

We must get it clear in our minds that joy, not gloom, is the birthright of a child of God, and is the natural fruit of a Christian life. We are made for joy, and if our lives are characterised by gloom there is something wrong. Joy is being blocked. When we clear away the obstacles then joy comes through – automatically. If gloom does characterise our lives then we should not look *around* for the cause – we should look *within*. John 15:11 points out that Christ's joy and our joy are not two different types of joy. They are allied, not alien. *'My* joy may be in you and … *your* joy may be complete.' We are made in the inner structure of our being for His joy.

Lord Jesus, I am so thankful that Your joy can become my joy. Help me take my birthright of joy and live the life for which I'm made. Amen.

'The divine masterpiece'

FOR READING AND MEDITATION
EPHESIANS 3:1–6

'... the mystery of Christ, which was not made known to men in other generations ...' (vv.4–5)

Another of God's great surprises is the Christian Church. The revelation of the Church was not given to the Old Testament saints for it was a mystery that was hidden from previous generations. In Christ the Jewish theocracy is terminated and replaced by a new international community – the Church. What a surprise it must have been to the Jews of Paul's day to discover that Gentile and Jewish Christians were now heirs of the same blessing, members of the same Body, and partakers of the same promise of salvation. Tom Rees, a famous Welsh preacher, described the Church as 'the divine masterpiece'. It is. Through it God accomplishes His highest purposes. Nothing in earth or heaven can equal it.

Father, enlarge my vision of Your Church. I am so grateful that I am a part of it. Amen.

An 'open' secret

FOR READING AND MEDITATION
ROMANS 16:17–27

'... according to the revelation of the mystery hidden for
long ages past ...' (v.25)

I n English a 'mystery' is something dark, obscure,
puzzling, even incomprehensible. The Greek word
mysterion, however, denotes a secret – something too
profound for human reasoning – but it is one that can
be divulged, especially to the initiated. It is an esoteric
'mystery' reserved for the spiritually elite. The word
in its original setting had to do with secret rites and
initiations, and was used in connection with the secret
teachings of the many mystery religions of the world at
that time. The 'mystery' of the Church, then, is a truth
which is beyond human discovery, but which has been
revealed by God and now belongs to the whole Church.
The 'secret' has been made open. And how!

*O Father, how can I thank You enough for sharing this 'open
secret' with me? I am grateful beyond words that I am a
part of Your Church. Amen.*

A false hope

FOR READING AND MEDITATION
1 CORINTHIANS 10:23–33

'Do not cause anyone to stumble, whether Jews, Greeks or the church of God …' (v.32)

The Church is not the whole of Christendom as so many believe. Ever since AD 313, when Constantine proclaimed Christianity the favoured religion of the Roman Empire, there has existed what is known as 'Christendom' – that is, the realm or domain of the 'christened'. Whatever we might think about the act of christening, it is a false hope that it automatically makes one fit to enter heaven. A Cambridge professor used to say, 'When I was a child I was both christened and vaccinated, but I am afraid that neither of them took.' That, unhappily, reflects the state of multitudes today. They have been christened but not Christened; baptised as infants but not born again as adults.

O God, rouse us to clarify this issue before millions more go into eternity resting on a false hope. Amen.

Called!

'And you also are among those who are called to belong to Jesus Christ.' (v.6)

T he *Shorter Westminster Catechism* defines the Church in this way: '… the whole number of the elect that have been, are, or shall be gathered into one under Christ, the Head thereof, and is the spouse, the body, the fullness of Him that filleth all in all.' The Greek word for Church is *ekklesia*, and means a people who are 'called out' – called out from the world because they belong to the Lord. Karl Barth, the well-known theologian, graphically described the Church in this way: 'The Church is like a company of citizens, rushing from everywhere – called out by the trumpet of God.' Christians are men and women who have been called out of the world to give their allegiance to the Son of God.

Yes, dear Father, I have heard and answered Your call and my heart responds, not in pride, but humility. What a privilege. What a destiny. Amen.

One Body

FOR READING AND MEDITATION
I CORINTHIANS 12:12–26

'For we were all baptised by one Spirit into one body ...'
(v.13)

The Bible does more than define the Church, it also describes it. 'The Church' is mentioned more than a hundred times in the New Testament, and is portrayed by many different images. The Bible does not say anything about images *in* the Church, but it abounds with images *of* the Church. It is pictured as a body, a temple, a bride, a mother, a family, a fold, salt, a loaf, a garden, a pillar, an army, a colony and a city. Paul's favourite figure of the Church, and no doubt the most powerful, is that of a body, and in the New Testament no one but he uses it. The Christian Church is a great Body made up of a lot of people who must all function properly if the Body is to be kept healthy and its work done.

Father, as part of Your Body, all that I have is at Your disposal. You know the needs of Your Body, the Church. Please use me to help meet those needs. Amen.

'His bright design'

FOR READING AND MEDITATION
EPHESIANS 1:1–14

'For he chose us in him before the creation of the world …'
(v.4)

Differing views are expressed by Bible teachers as to exactly where and when the Church began. Some trace its origin to the nation of Israel, stemming from the call of Abraham, others say with John the Baptist or even the apostle Paul. Most Christians, though, believe the Church was founded on the Day of Pentecost. Whatever our views about when and where the Church was first formed, the truth is that the Church began not in time but in eternity. Today's text tells us we were chosen in Christ 'before the creation of the world'. The Church is not an afterthought, not a by-product of redemption, but rather a forethought. It is, as one preacher expressed it, 'His bright design from the very beginning.'

Father, what comfort it gives me to know that You planned my salvation before time began. I am not Your afterthought, but Your forethought. Amen.

'A river as great as this'

FOR READING AND MEDITATION
2 THESSALONIANS 2:13–17

'… from the beginning God chose you to be saved …' (v.13)

In 1550, the Spanish explorer Vincente Pinzon sailed into the mouth of what we now call the Amazon River. He declared, 'A river as great as this must drain a continent!' and it was eventually traced to its source in the Andes. We trace the Jewish nation all the way back to Abraham. We trace the human race all the way back to Adam and Eve. But if we want to trace the beginning of the Christian Church we must step off the platform of time. Paul traces the Church all the way back to the heart of God. Somewhere in the mists of eternity, deep in the heart of God, we find our eternal destiny was settled in the Lamb slain before the foundation of the world. Always remember, God had a Lamb before He had a man.

Father, how thrilling it is that You anticipated the fall of Your human creation and prepared in advance the great plan of salvation. Amen.

Why He framed the world

FOR READING AND MEDITATION
EPHESIANS 3:7–21

'His intent was that now, through the church, the manifold wisdom of God should be made known …' (v.10)

One Welsh theologian declared, 'He framed the world that He might form the fellowship.' The creation of the world, and all that relates to it, was effected in order that God might bring out of it His masterpiece, the Church. God knew before He created Adam and Eve that they would succumb to the devil's temptation. Yet He went ahead because He had prepared another plan that would remain secret until the day of the apostle Paul that would result in even more glory being brought to Himself. Adam and Eve started out in innocence, but they failed. We start out in sin, and we are going to make it to heaven – not, of course, in our own strength, but through the mercy and the grace of God.

Gracious and loving Father, I see so clearly that sin is no match for Your wisdom, and that Your grace and power are awesome. Amen.

A joy for ever

FOR READING AND MEDITATION
REVELATION 21:9–27

'Come, I will show you the bride, the wife of the Lamb.' (v.9)

Sir Christopher Wren, the architect of St Paul's Cathedral, chose on his retirement to live in Camberwell, where it was possible to view the cathedral, the construction of which had been his crowning glory. Wren lived to 90 years of age, and sometimes sat with a small telescope in his hand, looking out across the Thames and surveying with pleasure and pride the cathedral he had designed – the master contemplating his masterpiece. One day in the future, when the Church is complete, something similar will take place in heaven: the Master will contemplate His masterpiece – the Church. One of the greatest sights in heaven will be the Master – Christ – contemplating His masterpiece: the Church.

Lord Jesus Christ, to be saved from hell would be enough, but to be a part of Your masterpiece is more than my mind can take in. Amen.

God's greatest surprise

*'No-one has ever seen God, but God the One and Only …
has made him known.' (v.18)*

God's greatest surprise ever is His coming to this world in the Person of His Son. How it must have staggered Jewish minds to be faced with the truth which John delineates so beautifully in the verses we have read today, namely that the 'Word', whom he declares 'was *with* God' and '*was* God' (v.1), took on human form and lived among us. They would never have conceived of the 'Word' as a separate entity. Our Lord, while never ceasing to be what He had always been – true God – became what He had never been before – true man. Amazing and incredible though it may be, this truth is the very heart of our faith. Indeed, it is impossible for a person to receive God's gift of salvation without acknowledging it.

O God my Father, I am so grateful that when we couldn't come to You, You came to us. Your incarnation is my salvation. Amen.

'Too wonderful for words'

FOR READING AND MEDITATION
1 JOHN 1:1–10

'We proclaim to you what we have seen and heard …' (v.3)

The New Testament writers struggled to put the fact of the incarnation into words. Paul says in 2 Corinthians 9:15, 'Thank God for his Son – his Gift too wonderful for words' (TLB). In four statements involving three of the physical senses – hearing, sight, touch – John endorses the fact that the Word actually did become flesh. If God had not come in the flesh then our salvation would not have been possible. Jesus had to be made like us in order to save us because, in the words of Bishop Handley Moule, 'A Saviour who is not wholly God and wholly man would be like a bridge broken at one end.' Let every person gasp at such a mystery. Jesus is the heart of God wrapped in human flesh.

O Father, the unveiling of the heart of Jesus helps me see what is back in eternity. What mercy. What humility. What grace. Amen.

Never to be repeated

FOR READING AND MEDITATION
ISAIAH 7:1–14

*'The virgin will be with child and will give birth to a son,
and will call him Immanuel.' (v.14)*

Let there be no mistake about it, the centre of the
Christian faith is the incarnation – God becoming
man. Other matters are important, but this is the central
issue. Some time ago I watched a television programme
featuring a group in India who were trying to groom their
swami to be a reincarnation of Christ. What complete
nonsense. Christ is utterly unique and became incarnate
once – and once only. Nothing like it had happened
before and nothing like it will happen again. By its very
nature the incarnation was the event of all events – the
most surprising event in all history. And never to be
repeated.

*Father, I am so thankful that Your incarnation is the
complete and total answer to human needs. No repetition
is needed. Amen.*

The gospel sureties

FOR READING AND MEDITATION
1 JOHN 4:1–21

'Every spirit that acknowledges that Jesus Christ has come in the flesh is from God …' (v.2)

To the heretic Gnostics, the idea of the incarnation – of the Word becoming flesh – was abhorrent. So to them Jesus was not God become man, but the revealer of knowledge which would bring salvation. The first letter of John was written mainly to combat this falsehood. John tells us that one way to discover if someone is speaking by the Holy Spirit is to ask them whether or not they believe that Jesus Christ has come in the flesh – that He actually became a man. Our salvation hinges on Jesus being God incarnate – not merely a moral teacher, an inspiration or a philosopher. That, to John, was the great issue. Over against the vagaries of Gnostic speculation John set the vitalities of the gospel sureties.

Gracious Saviour, thank You that You were willing to come to earth as a man. Receive my praise. In Jesus' name. Amen.

Good news, not good views

FOR READING AND MEDITATION
I TIMOTHY 3:1–16

'He appeared in a body, was vindicated by the Spirit ...'
(v.16)

The fact that the Word became *flesh* is the very genius of the gospel. No other world faith has such a message. Take any non-Christian religion and all you will discover is a word become word. All other faiths claim that God has spoken to their founder, and to prove it they show us their books, in which often there are good and wholesome words. Christianity has a book too, the Bible, but one difference between this book and other religious texts is that it is a revelation: it unfolds the fact that God has come into the world in the Person of His Son. The Bible itself does not give us salvation – the Word become words – but the incarnation – the Word become flesh. Jesus is good news; all else is good views.

O Jesus, I look on You and know there is no other like You. You are God's only Son, and therefore the only incarnate One. Amen.

God takes a body

FOR READING AND MEDITATION
HEBREWS 10:1–17

'Sacrifice and offering you did not desire, but a body you prepared for me …' (v.5)

God, in the Person of His Son, entered into our human condition and wore our flesh. Some object to the idea that God took on a material body because they think that physical matter is in itself evil and God ineffably aloof. However, the seat of evil is in the will, not in matter. Of course, matter has been affected by the evil that came into the world through sin, but to root evil in matter, and not in the will, is an attempt to blame evil on something other than personal responsibility – a foolish but self-serving evasion. The Christian faith meets us where we are – in the flesh – and offers us redemption *in* the flesh, not *from* the flesh. We live for Christ in our bodies, not apart from them.

O my Father, I am glad that You do not despise anything You made. You made it for a purpose, and that purpose is redemption. Amen.

'Gasp in wonder'

FOR READING AND MEDITATION
MATTHEW 1:18–25

'… you are to give him the name Jesus, because he will save his people from their sins.' (v.21)

Archbishop William Temple explained: 'There are just two types of religion. The one type tries to meet God at the top rung of a long ladder; the other meets God at the lowest rung. In the one, men try to go to God, climbing up by their good deeds; in the other, men simply allow God to save them.' The message of Christmas is this: we do not have to climb a long ladder in order to reach God. He comes down the ladder to us and meets us on the lowest rung, and receives us there as sinners. Jesus, the 'Lord of lords and King of kings' (Rev. 17:14), descended the ladder to reveal God to us and to show us just how much God loves us. Everyone ought to reflect on this again this Christmas Day – and gasp in wonder.

Lord Jesus Christ, all things are Yours and yet You came down to earth in order to lift me to the highest heavens. Amen.

'In for a surprise'

FOR READING AND MEDITATION
MATTHEW 24:36–51

'Therefore keep watch, because you do not know on what day your Lord will come.' (v.42)

Our final consideration of some of the ways in which we are 'surprised by God' is looking at a surprise that is still in the future. I refer to the second coming of our Lord Jesus Christ. Jesus makes it quite clear that He will not come when we expect Him, otherwise He would not have instructed us to 'Watch'. There seems to be much misunderstanding and false teaching about the second coming of Christ in certain Christian circles. Some state quite categorically that He is not coming back. A number of years ago I was in a church in the USA and heard a preacher admit, 'I do not believe that Christ will ever return to this earth.' As I left the service I thought to myself, 'My friend, you are in for a great surprise.'

Lord, may I work as if You were not coming for a thousand years, but live as if You might come today. Amen.

More misunderstanding

FOR READING AND MEDITATION
PHILIPPIANS 3:12–21

'… we eagerly await a Saviour from [heaven], the Lord Jesus Christ …' (v.20)

S ome believe that Jesus has already come back. Those adopting this viewpoint fall into two broad groups. One group believes that Christ returned to this earth on the Day of Pentecost. However, they confuse the descent of the Holy Spirit with the descent of the Son. So many predictions of the second coming were made *after* Pentecost that they cannot have pointed *to* Pentecost. Others claim that Christ returned to this earth at the time of the fall of Jerusalem in AD 70, when the city was destroyed by the Romans. But as one more enlightened writer and theologian has pointed out, 'Part of Christ's purpose in coming to this earth is not to destroy Jerusalem but restore it.'

Lord Jesus Christ, Your first coming was foretold and fulfilled, and so will Your second coming be also. I believe and wait – with confidence. Amen.

An event – not a process

FOR READING AND MEDITATION
I THESSALONIANS 4:13–18

'For the Lord himself will come down from heaven, with a loud command …' (v.16)

Some say Christ will *never* come back, while others say He has *already* returned. A third view, which is equally wrong, is: Christ is *always* coming back. Frank Ballard, a writer who subscribes to this view, claimed, 'The coming of Christ is not an event, but a process which includes innumerable events, a perpetual advance of Christ in the activity of His kingdom.' The coming of Christ into human affairs, however, is quite different from the second coming, and with so many verses in Scripture affirming this, it is astonishing that any student of the New Testament could ever confuse the two. No, Christ's second advent is an event, not a process.

Father God, the coming again of Your Son to this earth gives a horizon and meaning to the whole of history. I am so grateful. Amen.

Is death Christ's coming?

FOR READING AND MEDITATION
JOHN 21:15–25

'Jesus answered, "If I want him to remain alive until I return, what is that to you?"' (v.22)

Another mistaken view of Christ's second coming is the belief that the return of the Redeemer is to be identified with the death of the believer. Clearly, the disciples interpreted Jesus' remark as meaning that John would live until the second coming. But John refutes this idea by explaining, 'Jesus did not say that he would not die; he only said, "If I want him to remain alive until I return, what is that to you?"' To equate Christ's return with death on the basis of this passage is to ignore the clarification made by John. And, what is more, in Philippians 1:23 the great apostle Paul makes it crystal clear that death is not Christ coming to the believer, but the believer going to be with Him.

Lord Jesus, the prospect that one day I will be with You quickens my spiritual pulse and moves me forward in glad anticipation. Amen.

As ... so

'This same Jesus, who has been taken from you into heaven, will come back in the same way ...' (v.11)

There is not the time or space to go into all the features of the second coming; my point here is simply to affirm that one day in the future our Lord will return to planet Earth. It is not the fact of His coming that will surprise expectant believers, nor even the manner of His coming; it will be the moment of it. The words uttered by the angels to the disciples as Jesus returned to heaven from the Mount of Olives, recorded in our reading today, indicate that as He went away, so He will come back. Jesus went away visibly; He will come back visibly. He went up from earth to heaven; He will come back from heaven to earth. He left from the Mount of Olives; He will return to the Mount of Olives.

Lord Jesus, You fulfil every promise made concerning You, and I know You will fulfil the promise of Your coming again to this world. Amen.

The last word

FOR READING AND MEDITATION
ISAIAH 40:18–31

*'"To whom will you compare me? Or who is my equal?"
says the Holy One.' (v.25)*

I wonder how many surprises the Lord has waiting
for you in the year that lies ahead. Learn to look out
for them, for you never know what God is going to do
next. It is possible to go through a whole year– or even
longer – missing surprises. But we can be sure of this:
God's surprises *will* appear in the coming year. So watch
out for them and don't let them slip away unnoticed.
His surprises make life a great adventure. Be ready for
whatever God has planned for you up ahead, and look out
for those times when you walk around some bend in the
road, or are struggling to find your way in the darkness,
and the Almighty whispers in your ear, 'Surprise!'

*O God, how can I thank You adequately for the surprises
of the past and the ones that are still to come? I await the
future with expectancy and joy. Amen.*

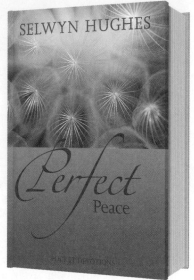

Also by Selwyn Hughes – *Every Day with Jesus*

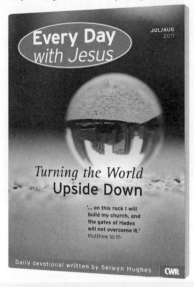

With around a million readers, this compact bimonthly devotional is
one of the most popular daily Bible-reading tools in the world:

- Get practical help with life's challenges
- Gain insight into the deeper truths of Scripture
- Be challenged, comforted and encouraged
- Look at six topics in depth each year
- Get more out of each issue with our free online extras for groups
  including video and discussion starters.

Individual issues: £2.75
Annual UK subscription: £14.95 for six issues (includes p&p)

Also available in Large Print Format and by daily email
Email subscription £13.80 per year

Courses and seminars

Publishing and new media

Conference facilities

Transforming lives

CWR's vision is to enable people to experience personal transformation through applying God's Word to their lives and relationships.

Our Bible-based training and resources help people around the world to:
• Grow in their walk with God
• Understand and apply Scripture to their lives
• Resource themselves and their church
• Develop pastoral care and counselling skills
• Train for leadership
• Strengthen relationships, marriage and family life and much more.

Our insightful writers provide daily Bible-reading notes and other resources for all ages, and our experienced course designers and presenters have gained an international reputation for excellence and effectiveness.

CWR's Training and Conference Centre in Surrey, England, provides excellent facilities in an idyllic setting – ideal for both learning and spiritual refreshment.

CWR Applying God's Word
to everyday life and relationships

CWR, Waverley Abbey House,
Waverley Lane, Farnham,
Surrey GU9 8EP, UK

Telephone: +44 (0)1252 784700
Email: info@cwr.org.uk
Website: www.cwr.org.uk

Registered Charity No 294387
Company Registration No 1990308